THE A-Z OF CURIOUS

ESSEX

PAUL WREYFORD

The History Press

First published 2013

The History Press
The Mill, Brimscombe Port
Stroud, Gloucestershire, GL5 2QG
www.thehistorypress.co.uk

British Library Cataloguing in Publication Data.
A catalogue record for this book is available from the British Library.

ISBN 978 0 7524 8986 5

Typesetting and origination by The History Press
Printed in Great Britain

This book is dedicated to Tommy and Avelina

Introduction

Oscar Wilde once quipped that people have 'an insatiable curiosity to know everything – except what is worth knowing'.

I must confess that what I have penned on the following pages may not necessarily be 'worth knowing' and should you, the reader, wish to go no further, it is unlikely to have a detrimental effect on the development of your intellect. However, the fact you are holding this book in your hands suggests Mr Wilde was right. There is no doubting that we do like to know about things we do not perhaps need to know about.

This is a book for curious people about all things curious in Essex.

My wife has always said I'm curious. I am the sort of person who needs to pop my head round that next corner, or to dig a little deeper below the surface. After all, you never know what you might find. And it is even more exciting when you find something you are least expecting.

Every county in England has its curiosities. Essex is one of the largest, and therefore it is no surprise that it should be home to so many curious tales, customs and people.

In the following pages, I hope even those who have lived in Essex all their lives will discover something they never knew about the county. Admittedly, as Mr Wilde remarked, it might not be worth knowing, but I am hopeful it will be of some interest and amusement at the very least.

Paul Wreyford, 2013

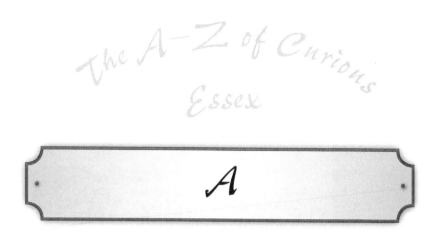

⚜ ABBERTON ⚜

All shook up

There is perhaps no better place to start a tour of curious Essex than with an event that shook the county – literally.

In fact, it shook most of the country.

Many people are not even aware that the UK has suffered from a severe earthquake. Even fewer know that the most destructive on record in England took place in rural Essex in 1884. The epicentre of the Great British Earthquake – as it is now known – was an area south of Colchester. Abberton Reservoir, the largest reservoir in Essex, now conveniently marks the spot on a map of the British Isles. It is said that every building in neighbouring Abberton and Langenhoe was damaged when the earth shook just before 9.20 a.m. on 22 April. It is fortunate that the epicentre was in what is still a very rural part of the county. Even today the villages of Abberton and Langenhoe are sparsely populated. There are often more visitors than residents. The reservoir (built in the 1930s) is now a popular nature reserve, and still a haven of tranquillity.

It was far from tranquil when the earthquake struck on that fateful April morning, however. It is said that the tremor lasted some 20 seconds in Abberton. In those 20 seconds, more than 1,200 buildings were damaged within a radius of 150 miles. The shockwaves were felt over an area of 50,000 square miles, as far north as Cheshire and as far west as Somerset. The earthquake was even felt on the Continent in Belgium.

Locally, hundreds were made homeless and the church at Langenhoe was virtually destroyed. Some believed the earthquake to be a sign of the end of the world.

What is perhaps curious is that the number of people killed is much debated. Mercifully, there were only a handful of casualties, if any at all. Some reports at the time claimed there was no loss of life. However, others talked

It is difficult to believe that tranquil Abberton Reservoir now marks the spot where a shocking event in British history took place.

of a child dying after being hit by falling rubble, while a pensioner is said to have died of fright.

Today, quiet Abberton – with its reservoir now serving what is the driest county in England – seems the unlikeliest place in the world to have been the scene of so much devastation. It is perhaps no surprise that even some residents are blissfully unaware of what happened here more than 125 years ago. One can only assume that newcomers to the parish are a little shocked when they are told – though certainly not to the extent of those who experienced that incredible morning in April.

✤ ABBESS RODING ✤

The spy who loved Cromwell

It is no secret that one of the greatest figures in British intelligence was born at Abbess Roding, north of Chipping Ongar. However, few residents today are aware of the fact that Oliver Cromwell's celebrated spymaster spent his early life in their village. Even the name John Thurloe means little or nothing to most.

Some historians have suggested that the country has never had a more efficient or effective secret service than when Thurloe was in charge of intelligence. As Cromwell's right-hand man, Thurloe was one of the most powerful individuals in England.

Thurloe, who was the son of a former rector of Abbess Roding, was born in 1616. He took little or no part in the Civil War, but rose to prominence within Cromwell's government. Thurloe was the man responsible for signing the letters sent out to sheriffs ordering them to proclaim Cromwell as Lord Protector.

It was in his role in charge of the intelligence department that he earned his reputation, however. Thurloe was so successful in detecting and thwarting plots against the republic that it was remarked that Cromwell carried at his belt the secrets of all the princes of Europe. Thurloe was able to keep his master informed of all the plans of foreign governments. Thanks to his many spies and agents, he was always able to keep one step ahead of the enemy, of whom there were many. He uncovered numerous plots.

Thurloe even had spies in the exiled royal court, and it is said that Cromwell could tell Royalists returning from abroad what had been said to them during their secret interviews with Charles II himself. And even when the Royalists returned to power, many of the king's supporters were nervous, as it was said that Thurloe had information that would have sent more than a few to the scaffold as traitors.

Thurloe was arrested at the Restoration, but released on condition that he helped the new government when required. It is said that Charles II even offered him a similar position, such was his reputation, but Thurloe chose to retire from public life. He said he could never serve the new king, as he had done Cromwell, whose rule, he remarked, was 'to seek out men for places, and not places for men'.

Thurloe was devoted to Cromwell and remained faithful to him until the last. It appears he had little intention of helping the new government under Charles II, as, upon Thurloe's death in 1668, a false ceiling was discovered in his London home. Stored there were many state papers and intelligence reports; Thurloe presumably determined to ensure his many secrets went with him to the grave.

⁂ AUDLEY END ⁂

Too grand for a king
Visitors to Audley End – one of the finest houses in England – would think it was fit for a king.

It is still an enormous and spectacular property, even though it is now only one-third of its original size. Its first owner, Admiral Thomas Howard, 1st Earl of Suffolk, was determined to build the grandest house in the country, and he succeeded. However, even the king appeared to be of the belief it was just a bit too grand.

Howard became a national hero for his role in defeating the Spanish Armada. When James I created his earldom in 1603, Howard no doubt decided he needed a property worthy of a man of his status, and one that was big enough to entertain

Even King James found magnificent Audley End to be a little too lavish.

the monarch and his royal court. Building on his land near Saffron Walden started that same year, but the house was not completed until about 1614. It is said to have cost £200,000, including furnishings, which was a massive figure at the time.

It was also in 1614 that Howard was elevated to the position of Lord High Treasurer. He must have looked forward to showing off his new abode. James appeared to be a little shocked when he finally came to visit, and remarked that Audley End was too great a house for a king, but sarcastically added that it might do for a Lord High Treasurer!

No doubt James was already aware of the rumours circulating that Howard was in severe financial difficulties. The building of the largest private house in England had come at a cost. Soon Howard was struggling with its upkeep. Talk of corruption became rife and, in 1618, James relieved Howard of his duties as Lord High Treasurer when he was made aware of his misconduct in the Treasury.

Worse was to follow for Howard and his wife, who were accused of committing embezzlement, extortion and bribery in a bid to finance their extravagant home and lifestyle. They endured a short spell in the Tower for their misdemeanours, before being allowed to return to Audley End, where they spent their final days out of the public spotlight – and, needless to say, still in debt.

⁘ BEAUCHAMP RODING ⁘

The wise man built his church upon the hill

Parishioners at Beauchamp Roding have to trek quite a distance – uphill – to attend their pretty church.

There is a reason why their place of worship stands in its lofty (well, lofty for flat Essex) and isolated position some distance from the village centre. According to legend, Old Nick himself would not let them build it any closer to their homes.

When villagers decided to construct their church hundreds of years ago, they selected a more convenient location in the village centre itself. For the building materials, they decided to make good use of a great stone that lay on top of the hill. It must have been some effort to drag the huge stone down the hill to where the church was going to be built. However, it appears it was no effort for the Devil to move it back again, as when they woke up the next morning it was found on the exact spot from which it had been taken.

They must have been a determined lot at Beauchamp Roding, for they dragged the stone down again and retired for the night once more. Needless to say, when they woke the next morning it was back at the top of the hill. They must have hoped it would be third time lucky, for it is said they moved it again one more time, with the same result, before giving up.

Some wise villager – perhaps fearing for his back – probably came up with the theory that Old Nick was responsible for the strange goings-on, and who would dare argue with him? It was therefore decided that the church should be built on top of the hill at Beauchamp Roding, north of Chipping Ongar, and there has stood St Botolph's

The stone in the churchyard at Beauchamp Roding that caused a lot of consternation.

ever since. In the churchyard is a triangular-shaped stone embedded in the ground that is reputed to be all that remains of what was used to build the church.

This tale is not unique. There are numerous stories of the Devil interfering with building works, and the Beauchamp Roding legend echoes many tales across the land.

However, the less romantic have suggested that the hilltop location of St Botolph's (and other similarly positioned churches) was chosen as a compromise. With paganism still rife, those opposed to a Christian church might have insisted that such a building at least be erected on top of a hill – a once common place for pagan worship.

⚜ BILLERICAY ⚜

To be a Pilgrim
Visitors entering Billericay are often surprised to see a ship on the town sign. The town is, after all, quite a long way from the sea and not known for its maritime pursuits. However, that particular ship represents a vessel that is familiar around the globe.

Most know that the *Mayflower* took the Pilgrim Fathers to the New World, but not so many know that the treasurer of the voyage was from Billericay. Merchant Christopher Martin lived at The Chantry, a timber-framed building

Billericay may not be beside the seaside, but there is a good reason why the town sign includes a ship.

still standing in the high street. Under his leadership, a contingent from Essex is said to have met in his home on the night before they joined the ship. It is said that the *Mayflower*, having set off from Harwich, stopped at Leigh-on-Sea, and it was there that Martin and his associates, including his wife, boarded the vessel in 1620, having walked from Billericay. Martin was responsible for provisioning the ship, and flour for the *Mayflower* probably came from a Billericay mill.

The religious dissenters put their hope in a new land, where they would be free to worship as they pleased. Under the command of Christopher Jones, of Harwich, the *Mayflower* – after another stop at Plymouth – reached Cape Cod Bay in what is now Massachusetts. During the voyage, which took sixty-six days, one died and another was born. However, the dream turned into a nightmare and, within a few months, it is thought that about half of the travellers had died due to the harsh winter conditions. Martin and his wife were among them. It was a tragic end for a couple who had tied the knot in Great Burstead Church, just outside Billericay, so full of hope. However, they can at least claim to have done their bit in forming a little part of Essex in the United States that we know today. The new colony, despite the hardships, did survive and Billerica (the 'y' was seemingly lost when they crossed the Atlantic) was among the new settlements named after Essex towns. It still prospers today – another indication that Billericay is well within its rights to proudly display a certain ship on its town sign.

The Ghastly Miller

Those struggling to lose a few pounds might help themselves by following the diet of an eighteenth-century Billericay miller.

When he ballooned to a weight that seriously started to affect his health, Thomas Wood – nicknamed the 'Ghastly Miller' by locals – decided to do something about it.

Slowly but surely he began to perfect what he believed was the perfect diet. And being a miller, it was perhaps no surprise that the chief ingredient in his bid to shed the pounds was none other than flour.

Wood, who was born in 1719, was in his mid-forties when he became subject to all types of ailments, such as headaches, gout, breathlessness and rheumatism. He even suffered from vertigo – though he was so big, one has to wonder how he even managed to climb the stairs in the first place! Wood had no doubt that his problems were due to his love of food and drink. Determined to do something about it, he first cut down his intake of meat and ale. Slowly but surely, he eliminated various foods and is said to have given up drinking liquids altogether, the exceptions being the milk or water he added to flour to produce his own kind of dumplings. So keen was he to stick to his new regime, he carried his ingredients whenever he left town in a bid to avoid the temptation of going back to his old ways. It is said he lived on his homemade dumplings for the rest of his life, though he did admit to occasionally treating himself by pouring gin or brandy over his food – purely for medicinal purposes, of course!

It is believed the miller lost at least 11 stone, though he was too suspicious to sit on a weighing machine. His case became celebrated within medical circles after appearing in *Medical Transactions*, a publication of the Royal College of Physicians. The article by George Baker suggested Wood, to quote the words of the miller himself, had 'metamorphosed from a monster to a person of moderate size' thanks to his strange diet. People from all over came to Billericay to meet the celebrated nutritionist, and many were inspired to follow his diet in order to improve their own health.

Wood was in his early sixties when he died, a reasonable age for that particular era, and one that he may not have reached if it had not been for his healthy homemade dumplings.

Last stand of the rebels with a cause

If you go down to the woods in Billericay today, you won't be in for a big surprise.

Norsey Wood, on the edge of the town, is like most woods in England. It is a pleasant and serene place to spend a couple of hours. And few who walk among its trees have any idea it is reputedly the scene of one of the most savage massacres on British soil. It is here that the infamous Peasants' Revolt of 1381 was finally put to bed, according to tradition.

The revolt not only finished in Essex, but started in the county too – at Brentwood, where an angry mob, consisting of humble labourers and fishermen from the Thames-side communities of Fobbing, Corringham and Stanford-le-Hope, saw off those who had come to impose a new poll tax on them. Already fed up with their working conditions, riots ensued, and thousands from Essex and Kent joined the rebellion, marching towards London to demand action. King Richard II famously confronted the rebels and promised to meet their demands. When Wat Tyler – one of the leaders of the revolt – was killed, the peasants eventually dispersed, still believing the king would honour his promise. However, Richard – once he had gained the upper hand – later rode into Chelmsford and formerly revoked his earlier pledges.

The leaders of the revolt were rounded up and executed. The remaining rebels were hunted down and the last significant band fled to Billericay, reputedly to Norsey Wood, where they put up one last fight. However, it was not a fair battle and most now refer to it as a massacre. Armed with just the tools of their trade, the peasants had no chance against the powerful army of Richard, led by the Earl of Buckingham. It is believed that about 500 rebels – unable to put up any serious resistance – were slaughtered under the trees.

☙ BIRDBROOK ☙

I take you … and you … and you …
There are two people who lie at rest in the parish of Birdbrook who must have
known the wedding vows off by heart.

Martha Blewit and Robert Hogan, according to a memorial in the church, had
no less than sixteen spouses between them.

Martha, of the Swan Inn at nearby Baythorne End, was the wife of nine
husbands successively, the ninth one surviving her. The memorial records the fact
that following her death in 1681, the text for the funeral sermon was, 'Last of all
the woman died also'.

Hogan did not quite emulate her, but we are told that he – in 1739 – married
his seventh and final wife.

Birdbrook, situated close to the Suffolk border, is not the biggest place even
now. One can only assume that Mrs Blewit and Mr Hogan came very close to
running out of potential spouses.

☙ BOCKING ☙

Read all about it!
It does not take long for a book to appear following a momentous event.

Publishers and writers know the importance of seizing the moment. Topicality
usually sells, and it was no different in the seventeenth century.

Just a few days – some say just a few hours – after the execution of Charles I, his
'autobiography' had hit the streets. It became the book everyone wanted to read.
However, it now appears the doomed monarch was not the author. The *Eikon Basilike*
was a sensational forgery, thought to have been the work of an Essex clergyman.

John Gauden was the dean of Bocking, near Braintree, from 1641-60. It was
while in service here that he would have penned the book supposed to have
been written by Charles, who was put to death by the Parliamentarians in
1649. The *Eikon Basilike* purported to be the spiritual autobiography of the
long-suffering king, written in prison during his final days as he awaited his
fate. Set out in the form of a diary, the work consists of a series of prayers and
meditations. Charles comes across as being a pious man of integrity and honour,
even a martyr and victim of a cruel enemy. That is exactly the image the author
wanted to portray. Gauden, himself a Royalist, produced the book in an attempt
to sympathise with the wronged monarch and rouse the people against the
Parliamentarians. It was a successful piece of Royalist propaganda, running into
several editions. For many years people believed the book had been written by
Charles. It was not until the Restoration – when Charles II came to the throne

– that Gauden claimed authorship. It was time for him to personally profit from his masterpiece. He believed he was entitled to a reward from the Royalists for his efforts in championing their cause.

Gauden, who was born the son of an Essex clergyman in 1605, became a bishop at the Restoration, but the see at Exeter was not a lucrative one. He eyed one of the top jobs such as Winchester. So, in 1661, it is said Gauden announced it was he who had produced the *Eikon Basilike* following the death of Charles. Sadly for Gauden, it only earned him the bishopric of Worcester, and not Winchester, and he did not have much time to reap any subsequent rewards anyway. By the end of 1662 he was dead, though he at least went to the grave having achieved posthumous fame. Had he not admitted he was the author of one of the greatest forgeries in British history, the name of John Gauden would be even less familiar than it is now.

⚜ BORLEY ⚜

The most haunted house in England

You expect a building that has stood for centuries to have a few ghost stories attached to it.

In contrast, you do not expect a new-build to have much paranormal activity. So it is something of a mystery how a property in a rural Essex village – which stood for less than eighty years – became known as the most haunted house in England. So famous did Borley Rectory become, it is said that it inspired more books to be written on psychical research than any other place in the world.

Borley is a small and remote village situated close to the Suffolk border. It consists of a few houses and a church. It does not even appear to have had a very eventful history and yet its name became famous. Think of Borley and you think of its ghosts.

The rectory was built in 1863 for the Revd Henry Bull and his family. It was not long before he reported some paranormal activity. And by the time he and his son had died, the house must have already had something of a reputation, as it is said that many prospective clergymen turned down the chance to become rector of Borley.

The Revd Guy Eric Smith was brave enough to come in the late 1920s, and by all accounts was a sceptic. However, when he started to hear strange noises he decided enough was enough. He contacted a national newspaper, and famous ghost-hunter Harry Price was sent to investigate. Price first came in 1929 and claimed his stay was 'sixteen hours of thrills'. He was to return on a number of occasions at the request of subsequent owners and noted that, between 1929 and 1932, more than 2,000 instances of paranormal activity took place at Borley Rectory. Price, not surprisingly, ensured he got a book out of it and Borley Rectory became known as the most haunted house in England.

Of course, it is perhaps no mystery why the property should achieve that status once the press and Price had finished with it. Even when it burned down in 1939 after its owner knocked over an oil lamp, many tried to put the blame on a ghost. However, a few still argue that there has to have been some foundation of truth in some of the many stories emanating from within those rectory walls. It does seem curious that a new building in an unassuming location should have been the centre of so much unexplained activity.

Spooky Borley gained fame with the help of a former rector.

The most common spooky sightings at Borley are that of a nun. It is said that during her life she attempted to elope with a monk. The couple were caught and handed the most awful of punishments. The monk was executed, but the nun was supposedly bricked up alive in the walls of her convent.

There is no evidence to substantiate the story – other than many reported sightings of a spectral nun – and some have even suggested the tale came from the colourful imaginations of the Bull children. If it did – and they innocently made up ghost stories to wile away the hours in their new home all those years ago – they would never have dreamed what it would ultimately lead to. Few properties with such a short life as Borley Rectory can have been associated with so much mystery.

⚕ BRAINTREE

A bitter medicine to swallow

Few feel the need to know the ingredients found in a bottle of medicine.

We swallow it and hope for the best.

That was probably the most sensible policy the patients of Braintree physician Benjamin Allen could have adopted. It is unlikely they would have wanted to know what exactly they were swallowing. If they did know, it is quite probable that they would have felt sicker than when they first went to see the doctor.

The former Braintree home of the eccentric Dr Benjamin Allen.

Allen, who lived in the grandest house overlooking Great Square, now home to Braintree & Bocking Constitutional Club, set up his practice in the town towards the end of the seventeenth century. It appears he was big on what we would now call alternative medicine. Of course, there were not many alternatives in those days, and general practitioners, if Dr Allen was anything to go by, would try anything in search of a cure – or at least their patients would.

Towards the end of his career, Dr Allen started to pen a commonplace book that listed his many remedies and cures for all types of illnesses and ailments. His treatments were probably seen as bizarre even in those days. It seems the doctor tried some out on his friends, one of which was famous naturalist John Ray, whose statue stands outside Braintree Museum. Dr Allen was also a naturalist and came to the attention of Ray when he announced that he had discovered glow-worms with wings. They became firm friends. Ray is famous as the father of English natural history. In his *History of Plants*, he described and classified thousands of species. It remained the standard work for some 200 years.

No doubt Dr Allen and Ray would have enjoyed discussing their latest findings of the natural world over the odd drink, though Ray might have thought twice about sipping anything the doctor put in front of him. It was half a pint of ale that Dr Allen recommended Ray drink when the latter was suffering from jaundice. The idea of a doctor encouraging someone to go down to their local for a swift half for the good of their health might seem a little strange. However, there was a twist. Ray was first told to soak the dung of a stallion overnight in his beer! It has to be said, he did afford himself the treat of adding a spoonful of sugar in the morning. It might not have been the most appetising breakfast but Ray was convinced it worked, and fortunately he reported that he only needed to repeat the dose once!

Dr Allen and Ray are both buried in the nearby village of Black Notley, Ray's birthplace.

A statue commemorates naturalist John Ray, a man not afraid to try anything once.

The unfunny man who wrote the first funny play

It is perhaps ironic that sixteenth-century playwright Nicholas Udall should have penned what is regarded to be the first English comedy.

On the surface – if you go by his reputation – this former vicar of Braintree does not appear to have been a bundle of laughs. As headmaster of Eton College, Udall was known as the 'flogging master' for his zeal in punishing pupils deemed to have

The 'flogging master' of Eton was also vicar of St Michael's Church in Braintree.

overstepped the mark. Essex poet Thomas Tusser, a student at the time, made a point of recording the fact that Udall dished out some harsh treatment. He ruled with the rod and Tusser claimed he was personally flogged for no reason.

One hopes that Udall was a little more forgiving when he was caring for his parishioners at Braintree. He was vicar of St Michael's Church from 1537-44. It seems he managed to combine the role with his post at Eton, as he was headmaster there from 1534-41/2. Whether or not he was forgiving of his congregation's sins, it appears they were certainly forgiving of his. They were not only deprived of their vicar when he was at Eton, but for almost a year when he was forced to leave that establishment, having himself been a very 'naughty boy'. Udall was brought before the Privy Council accused of colluding with two pupils who had been charged with stealing silver from the school chapel. He denied the allegation, but admitted what was considered an even worse crime: it is said that he was dismissed for homosexual practices. It landed Udall almost a year in prison. He was lucky, having been spared capital punishment, the usual fate for those found guilty of the practices he had confessed to. No doubt many a former pupil in his charge – the victim of his corporal punishment – would have wished they had been treated as lightly.

Udall was given a second chance by the people of Braintree, remaining vicar following his release from jail. Freed of his post at Eton, he would have presumably found a bit more time to serve them and to write as well. It is not known when his famous play *Ralph Roister Doister* – accepted as the first English comedy – was penned.

After leaving his Braintree position, Udall – despite his dubious past – became headmaster of Westminster School in the mid-1550s. One can only hope his own misdemeanours and resultant punishment made him a little more forgiving towards his new charges.

Nicholas Udall may have succeeded in making many theatregoers laugh, but it appears very few of his former pupils found anything funny about the author himself.

⁘ BRENTWOOD ⁘

The Martyr's Elm
Standing in the shadow of the famous Brentwood School is a memorial tree.

It marks the spot where Protestant martyr William Hunter was executed in 1555.

It is perhaps ironic that it should be so close to the seat of learning founded by Sir Anthony Browne, who once resided at nearby Weald Hall, South Weald. The school may be the legacy he would like people to remember him by, but the tree standing close to the main entrance is a visible reminder of his darker side.

Browne was an active persecutor of 'heretics' during the reign of Mary I, the Catholic monarch who gained the nickname 'Bloody Mary'. And he played a big part in the death of the teenage Hunter, who was cruelly executed for refusing to recant his religious beliefs. As the local magistrate, Browne interrogated Hunter when the latter was caught reading an English translation of the Scriptures, something that was illegal at the time.

There is a stone memorial to Hunter in the high street at Brentwood, but the tree is perhaps a more fitting one. The current tree stands on the spot where an elm tree once grew. It is said that the elm started to grow following the death of Hunter, on the exact spot where he was put to death. It was known as the Martyr's Elm.

Some have even suggested Browne founded Brentwood School to ease his conscience. In doing so he improved the lives of many, but a tree that now flourishes within its shadow is a reminder of a life that he played a big part in taking away.

❧ BRIGHTLINGSEA ❧

The vicar who made sure mariners saw the light

One would not be surprised if the people of Brightlingsea were scared out of their wits when they first noticed a mysterious light coming from the church tower.

And it would always appear on the darkest and stormiest nights.

However, it probably did not take them long to realise it was no apparition, or even smugglers signalling to their colleagues at sea – it was their own vicar.

The Revd Arthur Pertwee was not up to any mischief. In fact, he was carrying out a noble service. Not content to merely pray for those at sea after dark, the vicar would climb the steps of the tower of his church with a lantern in his hand. It was not uncommon, before lighthouses were in existence, for people to stand on a hill and light a fire to help guide sailors to safety. And, in Brightlingsea, you cannot get much higher than the tower of All Saints' Church, which reaches a height of almost 100ft. It is said that Revd Pertwee, who came to the parish in the 1870s, continued to climb the tower with his lantern well into old age. One can only wonder how many lives his selfless act may have saved.

Those who did not make it back home safely are commemorated in the church itself, with one of the most curious and novel memorials you will find. There are more than 200 ceramic tiles commemorating parishioners lost at sea. The Revd Pertwee started the memorial when a high number of Brightlingsea fishermen were lost in storms. Other tiles were added over the years, and the practice continued long after Revd Pertwee had himself passed on to other shores.

The tree of life

John Selletto did not believe in God.

And, just before his death, he quipped to his mates that if he discovered he was wrong when he departed to the other side, he would send a sign to tell them. He thought the most practical way of doing this would be to make a tree grow out of his grave.

Selletto died in 1771 and was buried in the parish churchyard at Brightlingsea. Of course, most soon forgot about the vow he had made before his death. However, when a sapling forced its way through the stone tomb a few years after Selletto was laid to rest, his words came back to haunt the living.

The story became very popular and spread to other parts, people coming from far and wide to see the tomb of the atheist, who was now with his maker – or perhaps somewhere less appealing!

Sadly, the tree became unsafe and eventually had to be chopped down, but Selletto, or perhaps a higher being, had made their point.

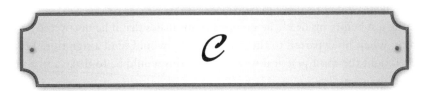

C

❧ CANEWDON ❧

The sign, the witch and the lock-up

Not many village signs have an image of a witch on them.

But Canewdon is not any ordinary village. It has long been associated with witchcraft, and some still say there is a coven of at least six witches here. They point to an old legend to back up that claim. It is said that the village will always be home to six witches – though some versions of the tale claim it is nine – as long as the church tower stands. It is said that every time a stone falls from the tower, one of the witches will die and be replaced by another.

Canewdon, a village north of Rochford, is often described as the centre of witchcraft in Essex, a county once full of witches if the notorious Matthew Hopkins is to be believed. He gave himself the job of rounding up 'witches' in the seventeenth century and hundreds are thought to have died at his hands.

The most famous witch of Canewdon was George Pickingill, who lived to see the twentieth century. This man of mystery has become a local legend and there are many tales of his exploits. His death also aroused much interest. It is said that on his deathbed he warned the villagers that he would reveal his powers one final time

The village lock-up at Canewdon still stands.

after his demise. Witches are supposed to have the power to control the actions of animals. Horses, in particular, can be moved by the will of a witch. At the funeral of Pickingill, one of the horses, for no apparent reason, is reputed to have broken away from its shafts and bolted.

In the shadow of the parish church at Canewdon still stands the village lock-up. Until Essex got its own police force in 1840, parishes were obliged to provide somewhere for local villains to cool off after committing their transgressions. Very few now stand, and the lock-up at Canewdon was unusual for the fact that it was big enough to hold three people, rather than the usual two. It is perhaps a fitting memorial to a village with a reputation for being a little on the dark side.

❖ CANVEY ISLAND ❖

Put up a fight
Fights outside a pub are nothing unusual.

They were particularly common at a famous Canvey Island hostelry in the mid-nineteenth century. However, they were not spontaneous alcohol-fuelled brawls. In fact, people could not get enough of them and they drew large crowds.

People once came to the Lobster Smack beside the Thames for a good fight.

The Lobster Smack, thanks to its remote location, gained a reputation for staging illegal bare-knuckle fights, some that reputedly lasted up to 80 rounds. Bouts took place in secret and only those in the game would know where the latest contest was going to be staged. The Lobster Smack was an ideal spot for the heavyweights of the day to have it out. Its isolated position next to the Thames also made it a popular haunt for smugglers in days gone by. The wide-open marshes ensured that any uninvited persons could be seen approaching in the distance. It is said that the bare-knuckle fighters used the pub as a changing room.

Some of the country's greatest fighters did battle here, including Tom Sayers, often regarded to be the greatest of them all. Ben Caunt was another legend of the 'ring'. Some claim that the bell of Westminster was named after 'Big Ben', as he was known to most. Caunt was forty-two and 17 stone when he fought Nat Langham in his final fight in 1857. He came out of retirement to settle a family feud and is said to have knocked Langham down in 59 of the 60 rounds. That was no mean feat, as Langham was reputedly the only man to have beaten Sayers. After 60 rounds, it is recorded that the exhausted Caunt and Langham finally shook hands, and the contest was declared a draw.

The Lobster Smack attracts many tourists today. It is thought that novelist Charles Dickens was thinking of it when penning the dramatic conclusion to *Great Expectations*. As Pip, Herbert, Startop and Magwitch journey down the Thames in their bid to bring about the escape of the latter, they take refuge at an inn for the night, Pip describing it as 'a dirty place enough, and I dare say not unknown to smuggling adventurers … for a more solitary place we could not have found'.

⚜ CHELMSFORD ⚜

'Razing' the roof

There is hardly a church in England that has not had to launch an appeal to repair a leaking roof at some point in its history. Fortunately, most are repaired before they collapse. However, that was not the case at the most famous church in Essex – the now cathedral of Chelmsford.

More than 200 years ago, the beautiful building that now stands proudly in the city centre was known simply as St Mary's Church. It did not become a cathedral until 1914 and, even today, it is reputed to be the second smallest cathedral in the country.

That it is still standing at all these days is perhaps something of a blessing. On a very memorable night in 1800, some columns collapsed and brought down the roof. What made this collapse so unusual was the fact that it was not through wear and tear, or any act of nature, but through the incompetence of some careless workers. Earlier in the day, it is said, some workmen were chipping away at the stone pillars that held up the roof. They retired that evening like they would have done any

Chelmsford Cathedral stands strong today, but that has not always been the case.

other day, no doubt satisfied at having 'successfully' completed another day's work. However, the town was woken in the middle of the night by an almighty crash. Daylight revealed the full extent of the devastation. The church no longer had a roof.

It is fortunate the incident happened at night, which meant there was no loss of life. One can only assume that those responsible were not among the onlookers surveying the desperate scene the following morning. They were probably long gone, but one hopes their consciences were stirred enough for them to at least contribute some loose change to any subsequent roof appeal.

A judge worth his salt

A statue of Nicholas Tindal stands in the centre of Chelmsford at the heart of Essex.

Talk to the many shoppers whizzing past and very few will have any idea what he did to earn such a prominent position in the county, or even who he is. To most who have little time or inclination to read the accompanying plaque, he remains a man of mystery, only his wig and gown giving more than a hint that he was a gentleman of the law.

However, Nicholas Conyngham Tindal is worthy of such a prominent position in the city centre as he was once a national hero. As a lawyer, Tindal won the hearts of the nation for his role in clearing the name of a queen in what became one of the biggest scandals in British royal history.

In 1820, Tindal successfully defended Caroline, the estranged wife of George IV, on charges of adultery brought by the king himself in a bid to divorce her. Their arranged marriage was not a success to say the least. When George set eyes on Caroline of Brunswick, he believed her to be coarse and even accused her of smelling. In fact, in his eyes, she was a figure of disgust. It was not long before they lived apart and did their best to avoid even seeing each other. It was certainly not a royal marriage made in heaven.

Caroline had a reputation for fast living, and rumours of a life of debauchery soon circulated. George, on becoming king, knew he could only divorce Caroline by proving she was guilty of adultery. His wife was brought to trial, much to the disgust and anger of the nation. Both the public and, more importantly, the press

stood up for Caroline. She was seen as the innocent party and George had already become a much-vilified figure. The people were so angry that riots ensued throughout the country.

Tindal was successful in clearing Caroline of the charges. The nation went wild. Impromptu celebration parties were held and Tindal was hailed a hero.

Judge Tindal was also a great reformer. As Chief Justice of the Common Pleas – a post he founded – he was responsible for the introduction of a law we now take for granted. In 1843, Daniel M'Naghten attempted to assassinate Robert Peel. In fact, he only succeeded in killing Edward Drummond, Peel's secretary, who he had mistaken for the prime minister.

Judge Tindal, who takes pride of place in Chelmsford, once cleared the name of a queen.

There was little doubt that M'Naghten was seriously ill mentally and he was acquitted at the subsequent trial on the grounds that he did not know what he was doing and therefore was not responsible for his actions. The landmark verdict caused a sensation. Tindal was ultimately responsible for the introduction of the plea 'not guilty by reason of insanity'.

Another of Tindal's legacies is the defence (to murder) of provocation. Tindal argued that when a person was provoked to such a degree that any reasonable man would lose self-control, he could only be guilty of manslaughter.

It is not often that a legal figure is honoured with a statue, and few in Essex may even give it a second glance, but this son of Chelmsford, who was born in what is now Moulsham Street, is well-deserving. Those responsible for putting him in this prominent position – even if most Chelmsfordians do not have a clue who he is – should have no case to answer.

Murder, he wrote

It was at a Chelmsford inn that a very famous man decided to bump off a very famous woman. And two clergymen must share at least some of the blame for the shocking deed. It was they who gave the man the idea, if the story is to be believed.

That man sitting by the window in the Saracen's Head, which still stands in the high street at Chelmsford, was novelist Anthony Trollope.

One has to remember that these were the days before television. The great novels of the Victorian age were the soap operas of the day and readers spoke about the characters as though they were real people. The author was a regular patron at the Saracen's Head. One day, according to tradition, two clergymen entered with a copy of the latest instalment of what became known as Trollope's Barsetshire novels. One of them was quick to condemn one of the lead characters. He is said to have cursed Mrs Proudie and declared: 'I wish she was dead.'

Trollope overheard the man of the cloth and looked up from his table. He is said to have coolly replied: 'Gentlemen, she shall die in the next number.'

And that is why the dreadful Mrs Proudie finally received her comeuppance in *The Last Chronicle of Barset*.

A Titanic contribution to safety at sea

It is perhaps fair to say that the sinking of the *Titanic* was the making of a man who became the most famous resident of Chelmsford.

However, it almost put an end to him.

Guglielmo Marconi, pioneer of the radio, received an invitation as a special guest to join that fateful maiden voyage to New York in 1912. He had to decline the offer, as he needed to hurry to the United States a month earlier on other business. He still held a return ticket.

It has to be said that Marconi was already making a name for himself, but the tragedy elevated him into the national spotlight. The reason he received an invitation was because the *Titanic* was equipped with the latest Marconi wireless system. However, it had only been installed for commercial use, for passengers and the crew to send and receive messages. The idea that it might come in handy should there be a disaster of any sort was as unthinkable as the ship was unsinkable! Marconi had long believed that wireless technology was essential when it came to safety, but he still had trouble convincing others. However, that was all to change when the *Titanic* hit an iceberg.

The Chelmsford statue of Marconi, a man who profited from the sinking of the *Titanic*.

The fact that at least one third of the 2,000-plus people on board were saved had much to do with Marconi. The ship that came to the rescue had responded to calls for assistance that had been put out via the Marconi wireless system aboard the *Titanic*, a system that had been developed at his Hall Street factory in Chelmsford, the first wireless factory in the world. The principal finding at the inquiry following the tragedy was that all 2,224 people on board the *Titanic* would have died without that wireless system. It was not long before it became mandatory for vessels travelling to foreign ports to have wireless communication systems fitted. Needless to say, business at the Marconi Company took off in a big way.

In the summer of 1912, just a few months after the tragedy, the world's first purpose-built wireless factory opened in New Street, Chelmsford, Marconi having operated out of his nearby Hall Street premises from the end of the nineteenth century. The fact that the public had just been told Marconi was responsible for saving the lives of more than 700 people ensured the firm would never look back. It went on to become world-famous and, from within its walls, the seeds of radio and, ultimately, television broadcasting were sown.

⚜ CHIGWELL ⚜

What the Dickens did he mean?

'Chigwell, my dear fellow, is the greatest place in the world.'

So declared novelist Charles Dickens in a letter to a friend. And it is here he set part of his novel *Barnaby Rudge*.

Most are of the opinion that the Maypole inn – the setting for the start of the tale – was inspired by the King's Head in Chigwell village. Dickens, continuing to wax lyrical about the area, declared it to be 'such a delicious old inn opposite the churchyard'.

However, there was another pub actually called the Maypole at nearby Chigwell Row in Dickens' time.

The description of the pub in the first chapter of *Barnaby Rudge* suggests Dickens was thinking of the King's Head in Chigwell village, 'an old building, with more gable ends than a lazy man would care to count on a sunny day', when putting pen to paper. However, he positioned his Maypole 'upon the borders of Epping Forest' – a position the real Maypole at Chigwell Row occupied.

For many years the two pubs claimed to be the inspiration for the novel. It seems both had a valid claim too. Now it is generally accepted that Dickens simply placed the King's Head – 'a very old house' with its 'huge zig-zag chimneys' – on the site of the real Maypole, as he deemed one to be the perfect building and the other to be the perfect location, with the perfect name too, in which to open his tale.

Today people may not share Dickens' view that Chigwell is the greatest place in the world, but many do like it, as the area is now a hotbed for the rich and famous.

Interestingly, Dickens believed the 'dullest' place in the world was also in Essex – the county town of Chelmsford.

The King's Head was not the only Chigwell pub to inspire Charles Dickens.

The 'unworthy' vicar of Chigwell

Chigwell may be home to the rich and famous, but there is at least one 'unworthy' man lying among them.

It appears he considered himself to be that, at any rate. Most would disagree, however.

In fact, Samuel Harsnett accomplished much in his life. The former vicar of the parish held many top ecclesiastical posts and founded, in 1629, the famous Chigwell School that has produced some notable names in our history, including William Penn, the founder of Pennsylvania. Harsnett was vicar of St Mary's Church from 1597-1605 and is buried within its walls. His memorial is reputed to be the only remaining brass of an archbishop in full regalia.

People still chuckle when they think of the epitaph of Harsnett. He must have been a very humble man to have believed he was so 'unworthy'. Perhaps Charles Dickens, a visitor to the village, used him as the inspiration for his infamous Uriah Heep, who was himself 'ever so humble'!

The memorial of Harsnett reads: 'Here lies Samuel Harsnett, formerly vicar of this church, first the unworthy Bishop of Chichester, next the more unworthy Bishop of Norwich, and finally the most unworthy Archbishop of York …'

It has, no doubt, often been said that this was a High Churchman with a very low opinion of himself. Harsnett had many Puritan enemies – and it is safe to say they would not have chosen any more suitable words for his curious epitaph.

❧ CLACTON-ON-SEA ❧

The day Churchill dropped by

Strollers on the promenade at Clacton-on-Sea are probably too busy taking in the view to notice a memorial. A plaque informs the reader that none other than Winston Churchill was a visitor way back in 1914.

Of course, there is nothing unusual or curious in that fact alone. He was in the habit of visiting the seaside in his role as First Lord of the Admiralty. However, his visit to Clacton-on-Sea was an impromptu one and certainly not a pleasant experience. His arrival here could have even cost him his life, and who knows what would have happened to the country if he had not been alive to become prime minister.

Churchill was in a naval seaplane heading towards Harwich on Admiralty business. He preferred to fly whenever possible and had himself taken flying lessons, but – because of his important government position – was forbidden from flying solo. Despite his love of the air and reputation for keeping cool in tricky situations, Churchill must have been more than a little concerned when the plane developed engine trouble. It was forced to make an emergency landing, ditching in the water close to the pier at Clacton-on-Sea. Fortunately, Churchill stepped out of the aircraft perhaps shaken, but not stirred.

Winston Churchill made an unscheduled visit to the beach at Clacton-on-Sea.

Some of the locals did not appear to be that sympathetic to his ordeal, however. As he waited for a replacement aircraft, members of the suffragette movement bombarded him with abuse. It is not thought he stayed too long to take in the delights of Clacton-on-Sea!

Perhaps the experience also played a part in the Churchill family later choosing Frinton-on-Sea – and not Clacton – when they decided they needed a holiday home in the area.

⚜ COGGESHALL ⚜

As the 'Crow' flies
Coggeshall is not the sort of place you would expect to find a notorious gang of criminals.

Today it has a reputation for being one of the prettiest villages in Essex, attracting many a tourist. However, in the mid-nineteenth century it had a reputation for something much more sinister, and few would dare come here for pleasure.

The Coggeshall Gang was responsible for numerous violent crimes during the 1840s. Residents of Coggeshall and its neighbouring villages lived in fear of this ruthless and brutal gang of thugs. During one break-in, the occupants of the house were reputedly tortured over an open fire until they revealed where their money was kept. The mere mention of the gang sparked terror in these parts. What was particularly cruel was the fact that the gang usually targeted the elderly and vulnerable.

When the first crimes were reported, Coggeshall had just one constable. He also just happened to be a part-time volunteer. It is no wonder the gang got away with so much for so long. There was little to stop them. However, as the gang's reign of terror intensified, it appears the police devoted more time and energy into catching the culprits. Finally, in 1847, one of the gang was apprehended. It was the breakthrough the authorities had been waiting for. That

The much-photographed Coggeshall was once not so welcoming to visitors.

individual eventually provided information about the gang and its activities, with the result that a number of warrants for the arrest of certain individuals were issued.

It is said a man named Samuel Crow was the leader. Many gang members were caught, some trying to flee the country, but he proved particularly difficult to catch. On one occasion the authorities went to the Black Horse pub in Stoneham Street to question the landlord of what is now thought to have been the gang's headquarters. During a search of the property and surrounding area, Crow was spotted hiding in the roof space of a nearby building. However, he managed to escape. Such was his reputation, it is said he was finally caught when a sharp-eyed officer recognised him as he was attempting to leave the country on a ship. After a trial that gained much national attention, the authorities attempted to put Crow and many of his gang members back on a ship – but one that would transport them to a life of hard labour in some inhospitable place. However, Crow died in Chelmsford Prison in 1850 before he had the chance to taste foreign shores.

Every 'witch' way but win

It appears to have been third time unlucky for a widow named Common.

In what was one of the last recorded witch hunts in England, poor Mrs Common was tried three times for witchcraft in 1699.

In those days, the test to see if one was a witch involved binding the limbs of the accused and then hurling them into the village pond. If the defendant floated, they would have been declared a witch and hanged, for it would have needed some magic to survive such an ordeal. If the accused drowned, they would have at least had the satisfaction of being declared not guilty. It was what you call a no-win situation.

Mrs Common, a resident of Coggeshall, appears to have floated. One can only assume her accusers were willing to give her another chance – or two – to prove her innocence by drowning. However, she survived a further two dunkings.

It appears that three times was enough proof she was a witch. Her punishment would have been death by execution, but Mrs Common died before her fellow villagers had the chance to put a noose around her neck – perhaps being submerged three times in the chilly village pond had brought on her fatal bout of influenza.

Sorry I forgot your birthday

It is a good job people were not in the habit of sending birthday cards in the early seventeenth century. If they had been, a certain Mary Honywood would have probably had to send one almost every day of the year.

When she died in 1620 – then in her nineties – she had a staggering 367 descendants. They were made up of sixteen children, 114 grandchildren, 228 great-grandchildren and nine great-great-grandchildren.

One of her sons bought Marks Hall, north of Coggeshall. The manor house no longer stands, but it was a big property – and it would have needed to be. When the family moved there in 1605, Mary was already well into her seventies. The estate gardens are now a popular tourist attraction. There is a memorial to Mary in the parish church at Coggeshall.

Mary Honywood was prone to suffering from religious melancholia, and she sought help from many a man of the cloth. There is a story that claims that none other than famous martyrologist John Foxe was one of those who tried to bring comfort to her. Full of doubts – not helped by the fact that many fellow Protestants were being burned alive for their faith during the reign of Catholic monarch Mary Tudor – Mary questioned whether she was worthy enough to take her place in Heaven. On one occasion, her lack of faith and fear of her own sin prompted her to declare: 'I am surely damned as this glass is broken.' At the same time, she threw her wine glass to the ground. However, it did not shatter into tiny pieces, but bounced off the floor unbroken. It is said Mary took the incident to be a sign from God, and it helped restore her faith and hope in him.

❖ COLCHESTER ❖

Humpty Dumpty sat on not any old wall

It was not any old wall from which Humpty Dumpty had a great fall.

And he was not the egg-shaped figure of fun that we know so well thanks to his appearance in Lewis Carroll's *Through the Looking-Glass and What Alice Found There*.

Like many rhymes from the nursery, this particular one has a far more sinister origin. The wall in question was at Colchester – scene of one of the most famous events in the Civil War. Here Humpty Dumpty sat, himself responsible for much death and destruction before meeting his end. Humpty Dumpty was no mere mortal, however, but a huge cannon belonging to the Royalists.

It was during the famous Siege of Colchester in 1648 that Humpty Dumpty, the nickname for this highly effective weapon of war, was placed on the town walls that encircled the desperate followers of the monarchy. The Parliamentarians, under the command of Thomas Fairfax, had the Royalists surrounded and there was no escape. Not that they didn't try, and Humpty Dumpty did his bit before a similar weapon belonging to the Roundheads did for him. The wall he was sitting on came crashing down after a hit and Humpty Dumpty 'had a great fall'. As we know, 'all the king's horses and all the king's men couldn't put Humpty together again'.

The Royalists ultimately surrendered and, no doubt, the rhyme became a victory song among the taunting Parliamentarians who lived to tell the tale that is still told in many a nursery today.

The grass does not grow under their feet

A number of Royalists trapped within the town walls during the Siege of Colchester in 1648, like Humpty Dumpty, came to a sticky end.

Following their surrender, the Cavalier leaders Sir Charles Lucas and Sir George Lisle were executed. It is said that Thomas Fairfax, leader of the Parliamentarian army, offered them their freedom as long as they did not take up arms again. These brave men told him that they were unable to give their word.

At the Restoration in 1660, their execution was deemed to be nothing short of murder and a memorial was placed on the spot outside Colchester Castle where they met their fate. Legend has it that no grass ever grew on the spot where their bodies lay after they were shot.

The final words of Lisle are worth a mention for being probably the wittiest ever uttered by someone about to embrace death. It is said he told the firing squad to move a little closer. One of his executioners informed him they were close enough. The quick-witted Lisle replied: 'I have been nearer when you have missed me.'

Sadly for him, they did not on this occasion.

A hair-raising encounter with a witch

You can get some good bargains at the market. But a Colchester holy man got more than he bargained for some 500 years ago.

According to an old legend in these parts, a monk at St Botolph's Priory was sent to buy some fish. He went to a stall run by an old woman who the locals

St Botolph's Priory was once home to a monk who was to regret trying to outdo a local witch.

believed to be a witch. Keen to get the best price, the monk dared to haggle with the hag, but tempers became frayed to such an extent that the furious stallholder cursed the thrifty and stubborn shopper.

The monk did not need to inform his brothers what that curse entailed, for that night his attention was drawn to his head. He was no longer sporting the traditional hairstyle of a monk. Growing out of his once bald head were bristles of hair. Many a follicly challenged male might have deemed it a miracle and gone in search of the witch to get her to curse them too, but there was a snag. The hair only grew in two bands, which made the sign of a crooked cross.

Despite attempts to rid himself of his new hairstyle, shaving his head and pouring holy water upon it proved to be only a temporary solution. The image of the cross grew back each time.

It is said the prior himself ordered the arrest of the woman and she was apprehended on more than a suspicion of being involved in witchcraft. Her punishment was death by execution, though it is thought she died of some sort of fit before the sentence could be carried out. With her demise, the curse was seemingly broken and the cross never again appeared on the bald head of the monk. Needless to say, he was probably a little more careful when he next went to market to buy some fish.

The royal road leads elsewhere

One day in the mid-fourteenth century, crowds lined the streets of Colchester to get a glimpse of a royal visitor.

Edward III was coming, or so everyone thought. However, it did only turn out to be a mere glimpse and nothing more, and there is a story from old that suggests it was not even the king the people briefly set eyes on. Indeed, it remains a mystery as to whether the monarch did come to the town that day or whether he even had any intention of doing so.

Certainly, the royal court of Edward arrived. As was customary, a huge feast was prepared for the king and his entourage. People flocked to the streets in anticipation.

At last, the 'king' – or so everyone thought at the time – entered through the famous Balkerne Gate. There was no royal wave on this occasion and onlookers could not even see his face, as his figure was shielded by numerous bodyguards and officials. No sooner had he appeared than he was gone again, ushered out of sight of the ecstatic crowd. No doubt the locals expected him to reappear in a more suitable spot from which he could address them. Patiently they waited, but he did not return.

Finally, in order to get the frustrated and disappointed people to disperse, the residents of Colchester were told the king was not coming after all. In fact, it is said he never had any intention of coming. If he had, something else had caught his attention and made him change his plans. No doubt the fake king had been a decoy in the hope the people would have been satisfied by the fact that they had at least been in the presence of the monarch, or thought they had.

So where did Edward go if he did not go to Colchester? What was it that drew him somewhere else? It is perhaps no surprise that most are of the opinion it was a woman, a very beautiful one, by all accounts. It was rumoured that the king had been lured to Boxted Hall, home of an important dignitary. It is said the dignitary's wife still had lots of fun when her spouse was away on official business. It is more than probable that Edward had noticed her in his royal court and liked what he saw. And so, it is said, Edward III did come to the Colchester area that day, but not on royal business. And he did rest his head within the county that night, but it was at Boxted Hall and not in the bed prepared for him in the old Roman city. If the story is true, you can be sure the owner of Boxted Hall was not at home that evening. It is perhaps safe to assume he was one of the dignitaries the king had left waiting in Colchester!

Jumbo is no white elephant

To outsiders it is probably something of a mystery why Colchester residents are so protective of the deteriorating water tower that stands close to the famous Balkerne Gate.

Enter through that 'gate' – once an entrance to the former walled Roman city of Camulodunum – and you cannot miss what some might regard to be a blot on the landscape. Many say it is not the greatest first impression of a town that is reputed to be the oldest recorded in England. It certainly is not the prettiest

'Jumbo' towers above Balkerne Gate in Colchester.

structure in a place that oozes history and is blessed with Roman remains around almost every corner. That was certainly the view of a local clergyman when it was built in the 1880s. He gave the tower the nickname 'Jumbo', not out of affection, but as a term of derision, as he did not like the fact that the monster building dwarfed his rectory and blocked all the light.

Now no longer needed for the purpose it was built, there have been calls for its demolition or for it to be developed. However, locals have grown to love Jumbo and regard it to be as much part of Colchester as the town's famous Roman walls.

In a rather strange twist of fate, there is now a campaign to save Jumbo, just as there was to save the very thing that the water tower was named after. The Jumbo the irate clergyman was thinking of all those years ago was a famous elephant at London Zoo. It was the star attraction until it was controversially sold to P.T. Barnum to join the 'Greatest Show on Earth' in New York. Jumbo had a mate in London and the public were horrified when they realised the two elephants were to be parted. People fought in vain to prevent Jumbo leaving British shores. There were questions in Parliament and even Queen Victoria joined the protests.

Now thought to be the largest surviving Victorian water tower in Britain, the campaign goes on to save Colchester's Jumbo in its original form.

There is another coincidence between Jumbo the elephant and Jumbo the water tower that campaigners have pointed out. Both were created in twenty months – that being the time the tower was built with some 1.2 million bricks, and that also being the approximate gestation period of an elephant.

A 'bleak' outcome

'Through deceit they refuse to know me.'

Those bitter words from the Book of Jeremiah became the epitaph of John Jennens and were inscribed on his gravestone when he was laid to rest at St Peter's Church in Colchester. Of course, that inscription cannot reveal the whole story, a quite remarkable tale that one of Britain's greatest novelists attempted to tell.

Jennens, who died in the second half of the eighteenth century, was a claimant in a famous dispute over the estates of William Jennens of Acton Place, Suffolk, who was the richest man in the country when he died, ironically having outlived many of the executors and beneficiaries of his will. The long-running dispute was the inspiration for Charles Dickens when penning the chancery suit of Jarndyce v Jarndyce in his novel *Bleak House*. Like Richard Carstone in the novel, it appears poor John Jennens never gained what he believed he was entitled to, and it seems he wanted to let everyone know just how bitter he was about it.

❧ CRESSING ❧

Mysterious knights were the order of the day
One can only guess what went on at Cressing Temple near Braintree hundreds
of years ago.

In fact, you have to guess, for no one really knows.

The estate was once in the hands of the powerful Knights Templar, a religious
order shrouded in mystery and secrecy. The activities of the warrior monks
aroused much suspicion, and that was to ultimately lead to their downfall.

The Order of the Knights Templar became the most famous Christian military
organisation of the Middle Ages. Initially formed to protect European pilgrims
on their way to the Holy Land, the Order grew to be a formidable fighting force
during the Crusades, with the result that it became very wealthy and influential.
Cressing was just one of thousands of manors the Order held across Europe, and
was also the first rural land in England granted to these particular monks. It is
believed that only a quarter or so were actually knights. The temple at Cressing
was founded in 1137 after Matilda, wife of King Stephen, gave the manor to the
monks. The Order itself was formed in France in about 1119.

It was Cistercian abbot St Bernard of Clairvaux who set out a code of conduct
for the monks, which included vows of poverty, piety and chastity. New recruits
had to sign over their wealth and land to the Order. The initiation ceremony
was particularly shrouded in secrecy. No outsiders were allowed to witness what
went on, arousing much suspicion and gossip. It is said that the monks consumed
their meals in silence, but only ate three times a week. No physical contact with
women – or even members of their own family – was allowed.

Cressing Temple became a self-sufficient and profitable estate, home to a
number of mills. Profits helped pay for the war effort in the Holy Land.

The Templars were known for their distinctive colours. The red cross on their white
mantles was a symbol of martyrdom. It was considered an honour to die in battle and
a sure guarantee of securing a place in Heaven. The Order gained a reputation for
bravery and as one of the most feared fighting forces in medieval times.

In the end, the Order of the Knights Templar became almost too powerful
for its own good. Many kingdoms were in debt to it. Among those that owed it
money was Philip IV of France. That has been suggested as one of the reasons
why he systematically attempted to wipe out the monks. Once the Holy Lands
had been lost, the Templars were no longer needed on the battlefield and many
questioned exactly what role they now played. Philip saw his chance to deprive
them of the power and influence they held over him. Rumours started to
circulate that the monks no longer kept their vows and got up to all sorts of
mischief behind their closed doors. Supported by Pope Clement V, Philip accused
the monks of all kinds of offences, including idolatry, heresy, witchcraft, devil

worship and obscene rituals. Monks were rounded up and tortured into making confessions. Many were burned at the stake, including the last grandmaster of the Order, Jacques de Molay, in 1314. He remained defiant until the end. According to legend, he called out from the flames that God would judge King Philip and the Pope for their actions, and warned them of a calamity that would come their way. Pope Clement died about a month later, while Philip was killed in a hunting accident before the year was out.

The persecution of the Templars was not so severe in England. In fact, Edward II at first tried to defend them, though he was soon forced to follow suit in condemning the Order. The English monks were arrested, but did not suffer at the stake as their French counterparts had done. With the disbandment of the Templars, many of the remaining monks were absorbed into other military orders, including the Knights Hospitaller – once the arch-rivals of the Templars. The Hospitallers – less powerful and secretive than the Templars – took control of Cressing Temple in 1312.

At its peak, the Order of the Knights Templar is thought to have had up to 20,000 members across Europe.

One of the treasured barns at Cressing Temple, once a place of mystery.

Visitors to Cressing Temple can still feast their eyes on two magnificent barns that stood when the Templars held so much power and sway. One of those is reputed to be the oldest timber-framed barn in the world.

Standing in the shadow of these magnificent structures that have stood for centuries, one can only imagine what went on within these walls and of those other buildings no longer standing. Many might insinuate what the Templars got up to behind closed doors, but it will forever have to remain a secret.

The secret knights at Cressing Temple aroused much suspicion.

❧ DANBURY ❧

End up in a pickle

You would not expect to find much more than a pile of bones if you opened a coffin laid to rest more than 500 years ago.

That is what Danbury residents thought they would set their eyes upon when they did just that in the late eighteenth century. However, when the lid was opened, there lying in front of them was the perfectly preserved body of a man in the vigour of youth that could have been placed there that very month.

The occupant is thought to have been one of three knights buried at Danbury. Their tombs are marked by three elaborate figures inside the parish church. One of those knights was disturbed in 1779 when a new grave was being dug. As they were digging, workmen noticed a big stone under which lay a lead coffin. With permission from the rector, the coffin was opened. However, it did not reveal a corpse, but another wooden coffin which, when opened, revealed a type of shell made of cement. When this was removed, the corpse at last became visible. Its flesh was white and its teeth in perfect condition, the knight's preservation due to a strange liquid that filled the coffin. Flowers, feathers and herbs lay on its surface.

It is believed that the famous Knights Templars were buried in an embalming pickle, which meant the occupant might have been a member of that particular religious order.

The coffin was sealed up again and returned to its tomb, no doubt ready to give some more unwary 'gravediggers' a shock in another few hundred years or so.

Great Scott!

If Walter Scott had not come to Danbury, it is quite possible he would not have penned his famous historical romances. *Waverley* – the novel that launched his fiction career – was 'reborn' in the Essex village.

Scott was earning a reputation as a fine poet when he came to Danbury at the beginning of the nineteenth century, but had not written any of the novels that eventually made him famous all over the world.

The reason for his visit was research. He had been asked by his publisher to complete *Queenhoo Hall*, a novel left unfinished when its author Joseph Strutt passed away. Strutt was born at Chelmsford, not too far from Danbury, which features in the historical romance. Scott is reputed to have stayed at the Griffin inn, which still stands on the hill at one of the highest spots in Essex.

Queenhoo Hall, the concluding chapters written by Scott, was not a commercial success. However, Scott explained in the 1829 general preface to *Waverley* – a work that first appeared in 1814 – that he owed a huge debt to Strutt and *Queenhoo Hall*. He suggested that *Waverley* would never have seen the light, had he not been called upon to edit the work of Strutt. Scott wrote that *Queenhoo Hall* 'evinced (in my opinion) considerable powers of imagination'.

However, Strutt was an antiquary and Scott felt the novel suffered because the author displayed his antiquarian knowledge 'too liberally'. He added that the language was too ancient and did not cater for the general reader. Nevertheless, *Queenhoo Hall* was the impetus Scott himself needed. He wrote: 'I conceived it possible to avoid this error; and, by rendering a similar work

Novelist Walter Scott is said to have stayed at the Griffin inn at Danbury.

more light and obvious to general comprehension, to escape the rock on which my predecessor was shipwrecked.'

Strutt had set his tale in the fifteenth century. The work highlighted the manners, customs and language of England at that time. Scott felt a more recent era – and a more dramatic setting – would fare better among readers. One perhaps cannot blame him. Essex – though Danbury is one of the highest villages in the county – cannot quite match the spectacular glens and mountains north of the border.

Scott had already started a novel before coming to Essex, but had consigned it to a drawer of his writing desk. After completing *Queenhoo Hall*, he decided it was time to retrieve it and *Waverley* eventually came to light.

It has to be said that *Queenhoo Hall* (and Danbury) was not the only inspiration for *Waverley*, but there is little doubt it played a big part.

❧ DEDHAM ❧

The painter who refused to be brushed off
At the heart of Constable Country – so named after one of Britain's most famous painters – lies the body of a quite different artist.

Most visitors to Dedham come to trace the steps of John Constable, who gained so much inspiration from the area. Constable's father at one time owned the mills at Dedham and Flatford, the latter just over the border in Suffolk now attracting scores of tourists thanks to John's famous painting.

Others come to see the school in Dedham where the young John was educated, or pop in at Castle House, once the home of Alfred Munnings, who was another famous artist.

Dedham is all about art, and yet few on the art trail take time to visit the parish churchyard. Here lies Tom Keating, the most important art forger of the twentieth century. Keating, who spent his final days at Dedham before his death in 1984, admitted forging about 2,000 paintings of some 100 artists during his prolific career. Oil paintings, watercolours and drawings purporting to be the work of the likes of Goya, Renoir, Rembrandt, Degas, Gainsborough and even Constable himself fooled the art world for years. He said he gave most of the forgeries away, but many also ended up on the walls of prestigious London galleries. Keating said he produced fakes to get his own back on the art world. He was of the belief that critics and dealers lined their own pockets at the expense of impoverished artists such as he.

Keating produced his own original works, but they never made any impact, prompting him to turn to forgery in order to prove his talent and ingenuity. Keating would often write a derogatory or cynical comment on the blank

Pretty Dedham was not only home to painter John Constable, but also to a man who fooled the art world.

canvas using lead white paint. It would then be hidden by the 'masterpiece' he went on to produce. He knew full well the works, should they be examined properly, such as by x-ray, would be revealed as forgeries. He even offered clues in the pictures themselves. He would sometimes use materials that were not available in the era his painting was supposed to have been produced, or include deliberate anachronisms.

Keating, who was born at Lewisham, started producing what he called his 'Sexton Blakes' – the Cockney slang for fakes – just after the Second World War. His enterprise did not come to light until the 1970s. When it did, it shook the art world. He was eventually arrested, but the case was dropped due to his bad health. However, Keating emerged from the court a hero to the ordinary man. He had succeeded in showing up the 'experts' and it made him a celebrity. The public viewed him as a loveable rogue.

In an ironic twist, Keating's fakes have themselves now become collectors' items.

Keating was buried in the churchyard at Dedham parish church. In that very building hangs a work from the brush of Constable himself, attracting many a visitor. Of course, we assume it is the work of that great painter … and not that of another!

$\mathcal{E}$

❖ EAST HORNDON ❖

Don't lose your head … or your leg

Do not be too surprised if you come across a couple of decapitated heads – and the odd leg – if you visit the now redundant parish church at East Horndon, south of Brentwood.

According to legend, this is the spot where Sir James Tyrell, of nearby Herongate, got the better of a serpent-type creature many centuries ago.

The beast is said to have escaped from a ship on the Thames heading for London after being captured from some distant land. It roamed the woods here, devouring all that came its way. The frightened locals called upon the lord of the manor to do something about it. Brave Sir James did just that. It is said he confronted the creature in the churchyard or thereabouts. He was a clever chap and had the foresight to fix a looking glass to his armour. As the serpent was busy preening itself with the help of its reflection – or possibly trying to impress what it thought was a potential mate – Sir James took the opportunity to cut off its head.

Sadly, the effort required in tracking down and dispatching the beast took its toll on Sir James and he died soon after his act of valour. That was not quite the end of the story either. The son of Sir James is said to have gone to the scene of his father's triumph and accidentally stepped on a sharp bone belonging to the remains of the serpent. He ended up with gangrene and lost a leg. The unfortunate one-legged son was depicted in a glass window at the church.

The Tyrells – a famous Essex family – appear to have been a clumsy lot. One of their ancestors is thought to have been Walter Tyrell, the man accused of accidentally killing William II. Out hunting in the New Forest, this Tyrell seemingly mistook William – known as 'Rufus' because of his red hair or ruddy complexion – to be a squirrel! Whatever really happened, the king was fatally injured by one of his arrows and poor Walter (though most believed he had done a great service in dispatching a much-maligned monarch) was forced to go on the run.

The Tyrells are said to have come to Heron Hall at Herongate after years in exile.

But what of that aforementioned second head at East Horndon Church? Well, that was the property of Anne Boleyn. After her beheading, it is said some of her supporters smuggled her severed head – other versions of the story say it was her heart – to her native Essex, where it was reputedly buried in one of the existing vaults at the Church of All Saints. It has never been located and could well lie here still, though it is not the only church in the country to make such a claim.

⚜ EPPING ⚜

Mary, Mary, quite contrary

Pity the men in the household of Mary Tudor who were given the job of telling the fiery princess she should refrain from celebrating Mass at Copped Hall.

No doubt they would have been filled with much trepidation.

Mary, an ardent Catholic, already had the reputation of being someone not to be messed with. Her Protestant half-brother Edward VI was on the throne at the time. Princess Mary – the daughter of Catherine of Aragon – remained fiercely loyal to Catholicism. She was forced to spend much of her youth as a virtual prisoner in various Essex palaces belonging to Henry VIII, as her father went through his numerous wives. In 1551, Mary was residing at Copped Hall, near Epping. It was not the first time she had been warned for celebrating Mass, a practice now forbidden under the new Church of England.

Robert Rochester, Francis Englefield and Edward Waldegrave were the unlucky men who drew the short straw. As important members of her household, they were summoned to appear before the Privy Council and ordered to tell Mary that she should cease celebrating Mass.

You can just imagine the party arguing among themselves as to who should be the one to tell the princess directly to her face. They knew she would not like it and were well aware of her hot temper. Indeed, when Mary learned of the order, she was furious. The trio – maybe through loyalty or fear – did not enforce the order, but that meant Rochester, Englefield and Waldegrave soon found themselves before the Privy Council again. Not only were they reprimanded for their disobedience, they were told to go back to Copped Hall and try again. It is said the men told the Council they would rather go to prison than relay the message for a second time. And they did. All three were sent to the Tower for their disobedience.

Edward decided he would personally deal with the matter. However, he was still a mere youngster and one can probably assume he also lived in fear of his big half-sister. Rather than pay her a visit, he decided to write her a letter. This time the big guns were sent to deliver it. A deputation led by none other than Lord Chancellor Richard Rich turned up on the doorstep at Copped Hall. It was soon sent packing. This time Mary told the party she would rather die than obey the king. It is not known if anyone dared take another message to her!

Fiery Mary Tudor lived at Copped Hall and few relished visiting her.

Mary got her revenge. After the death of Edward, she became queen in 1553. In a relentless bid to restore Catholicism, she put to death many of those who refused to follow her faith, earning her the nickname 'Bloody Mary'.

⚜ FELSTED ⚜

Hickory Dickory Dock

Many former pupils at the famous Felsted School have gone on to achieve great things.

And great things would have been expected of Richard Cromwell too.

As the son of one of the greatest Britons, Richard was expected to emulate his father Oliver, who led the Parliamentarians to victory in the Civil War and declared the country a republic in 1649. However, unlike his dad, Richard did not aspire to greatness and chose to go down a different path.

Four of the sons of Oliver Cromwell were educated at Felsted, the school founded by Richard Rich in 1564. Robert, the eldest, died at Felsted, a village north of Chelmsford, at the age of just eighteen, and is buried here. The second eldest son – also called Oliver – died in 1644, which meant that when Oliver Cromwell senior passed away in 1658, Richard was the eldest surviving son and was expected to take up his father's mantle.

Poor Richard was thrust into a position he had no desire to hold. He was the natural successor to his father and duly appointed Lord Protector. Richard Cromwell was now the most powerful man in the country.

However, Richard was very different in character to his father. He was weak and mild-mannered. While Oliver Cromwell has often been described as a lion, poor Richard Cromwell was frequently portrayed as a mouse – the legacy of this former Felsted schoolboy being a nursery rhyme. Nicknamed 'Queen Dick', 'Tumbledown Dick' and 'Hickory Dick', Richard Cromwell, knowing the people wanted the return of the monarchy, conceded power to Charles II. Richard became a figure of fun, mocked and taunted by his enemies. The rhyme Hickory Dickory Dock is reputedly a reference to his short reign. Richard is the mouse that returns from where it came from when the clock strikes one – symbolising a year in power, though he did not quite even reign for that long, just nine months or so. It is perhaps ironic that his father should have fought so hard to make the country a republic, only for his son to give it up without a fight.

One can perhaps sympathise with poor Richard. Sometimes sons do not take after their fathers. When he came to power, Richard had no military or political experience. It appears he had no desire to gain any either.

After the Restoration in 1660, Richard Cromwell retired from public life and ended his days a country gentleman, living in relative obscurity.

❖ FINCHINGFIELD ❖

The man who held his tongue for seven years
All of us must have at some point said something we have regretted during a fit of rage. It is not easy to control the tongue in the heat of the moment.

However, the eccentric William Kempe of Finchingfield, a village north of Braintree, was determined to do it. After he had lost his temper one time too many, he decided enough was enough. On this occasion he had accused his wife of adultery and soon regretted it. Being a holy and pious chap, he no doubt reflected on advice in the Bible that suggested a man was better off cutting out his tongue if he was unable to control it. Kempe never resorted to that, but he did vow that he would never utter another word to anybody for seven years as penance for the slanderous attack on his wife. And that is what the owner of Spains Hall, the grand house at Finchingfield, did. Nothing would get him to talk. Not even the death of Mrs Kempe in 1623 could persuade him to break his vow of silence.

It is believed that William Kempe actually died just as the seven years were up. Some have suggested his death was caused by the attempt to speak again. It is said that when he tried to talk, no sound came out of his mouth, so long had he remained in silence. It is possible he panicked and that may have brought some sort of seizure upon him.

There is an elaborate tomb in the parish church that gives the barest details of William Kempe's amazing – and perhaps costly – vow of silence.

✤ GALLEYWOOD ✤

Not a one-horse town

Take a stroll on Galleywood Common and you might spot the occasional horse and rider.

In days gone by, people flocked here to watch more than a few ponies being put through their paces.

It is sometimes difficult to believe that this haven for wildlife – an oasis of calm just south of the city of Chelmsford – was once home to one of the top racecourses in the country. It was also one of the longest circuits and certainly the only one in the land to encircle the village church!

The village sign gives more than a clue as to what used to take place at Galleywood.

There is a fanciful tale as to the origin of horseracing here, which started in the mid-eighteenth century, and as to why the parish church sat in the middle of the course. It is said that two sisters inherited a lot of money. One was pious and holy. She built a church. The other was not pious and holy, and out of spite she built a racecourse all the way round it!

There is no doubting that horseracing was a big event here. Meetings were usually held over two days. The gentry would come on the first day, while the labourers would come the following day. It became a big business. George III put up some prize money and thousands of people attended. By the late nineteenth

You can still see fencing from the former racecourse on Galleywood Common.

century, a new grandstand was installed. The circuit crossed the road on occasions and traffic had to be stopped during races.

Horseracing at Galleywood ended in 1935. There is still evidence to be found of those illustrious days – on the village sign, and in the names of pubs in the vicinity, which include the Running Mare and the Horse & Groom. Some of the fencing behind which the spectators would have stood is also still visible, while signs still request horse-riders – these days out on a more sedate trot on the common – not to stray from the course.

❧ GESTINGTHORPE ❧

'I am just going outside and may be some time'

In the top corner of the village sign at Gestingthorpe you will see a figure of a hunched man battling through a snow blizzard.

To the visitor it is at first a curious image. On a sunny day, this archetypal English village in rural north Essex is certainly a far cry from the inhospitable South Pole. However, it is in Gestingthorpe that one of the tragic explorers of the doomed expedition to the Antarctic – under the leadership of Robert Scott – spent much of his childhood. Few villagers of the time would have imagined that the frail boy, who suffered much ill health, would become a national hero. Captain Lawrence Oates will forever be remembered for his sacrificial death in 1912. When he realised he was a burden to his fellow explorers, he walked out into a blizzard in order to give them a chance to survive. 'I am just going outside and may be some time,' he told his friends. He was just thirty-two.

The family home at Gestingthorpe, a village north of Halstead, was Over Hall (now Gestingthorpe Hall), which stands close to the parish church. Oates was a child when the family moved here. It was during this time that the youngster developed his love for horses and learned how to master them. He was to join Scott's expedition on the back of his skill and knowledge of equestrian matters, being placed in charge of the ponies.

While the rest of the world was perhaps amazed by the courage shown at the South Pole by Oates, the villagers of Gestingthorpe would not have been. They would have been well aware of at least one other occasion when he was hailed a hero. Oates became a cavalryman and fought in the Boer War. He even acquired the nickname 'No Surrender Oates'. It is said that Oates, despite a bullet smashing the bone in his thigh, resisted calls to give up the fight. He successfully ensured that his men reached safety before making it quite clear to the enemy that he had no intention of giving up himself. At least he returned home on that occasion. His mother celebrated his homecoming in the restoration of the church bells at Gestingthorpe, to which she added an inscription praising God for his safe deliverance.

The hunched figure of Captain Oates battling through a blizzard can be picked out on the village sign at Gestingthorpe.

Oates eventually became disillusioned with military life, but, ever the one for adventure, he joined Scott in his race to become the first man to reach the South Pole. Sadly, Oates never returned on that occasion. The explorers did reach their target, but were not the first to do so. On the return journey, Oates succumbed to severe frostbite. His old wound gained in South Africa was also thought to have added to his problems. Presumably coincidentally, Oates chose his birthday to commit suicide, though he had already unsuccessfully pleaded to his companions to leave him behind in his sleeping bag. In Gestingthorpe Church records, it is stated that 'when all were beset by hardship, he, being gravely injured, went out into the blizzard to die in the hope that by so doing he might enable his comrades to reach safety'. Sadly, his sacrificial act was in vain as his colleagues later perished too.

Oates must have genuinely believed his fellow explorers still had a slim chance of survival and might have reached safety without him slowing them down. If that had not been the case, it is very unlikely that 'No Surrender Oates' – even though he knew there was little hope – would have given up.

⚜ GOSFIELD ⚜

Feast your eyes on this

Not many people can claim to have received a dinner invitation from a king. But the residents of Gosfield in the early nineteenth century would have been able to.

One of the neighbours just happened to be the exiled King Louis XVIII of France. He resided at Gosfield Hall from 1807-9 following the French Revolution.

It was a French custom to allow the villagers into the kitchen on a Sunday to see the dinner laid out for the monarch. And, on special days, they were sometimes afforded the privilege of watching him eat it! One can only imagine what would have gone through the minds of hard-up peasants as they watched the king rubbing his belly with satisfaction after polishing off a feast they could only dream of. It is a wonder it did not spark off the Gosfield Revolution!

However, Louis is said to have been a popular figure in his adopted village. There are tales of him throwing pennies (at least it was not scraps of meat) to the children as he passed through the streets.

Grand Gosfield Hall was the property of the Marquis of Buckingham. He sympathised with the Royalists of France and leased his home to the exiled monarch. Louis brought with him his full entourage. It is said his royal court consisted of some 350 people. The hall became the venue for lavish parties and a number of distinguished guests stayed here.

Louis moved to Hartwell House in Buckinghamshire after vacating Gosfield, a village near Halstead. Despite the troubles in his own country, Louis XVIII

Gosfield Hall was once home to King Louis XVIII of France.

appeared to live in style during his residency in England. At least he gave the people of Gosfield the chance to see a feast fit for a king – even if they could not enjoy any of it themselves.

⁂ GREAT DUNMOW ⁂

Whatever floats your boat
It is probably safe to assume that some people regarded Lionel Lukin as a little crazy – at the very least eccentric – when he 'played' with his model boats on the village pond at Great Dunmow.

Assuming there was not a craze in the late eighteenth century for what is now a popular pastime, it would have been a curious sight to see a grown man attempting to get his homemade vessels to float. He may have even been the butt of many jokes – particularly when his boats sank!

However, those who knew Lukin – and knew that he was not merely playing – would, no doubt, have applauded his efforts. People applaud him now, at any rate.

In those days, building boats that did not sink in extreme weather was not easy. In fact, no-one had managed to do it until Lukin. From his model prototypes – tested on the Doctor's Pond in the heart of Great Dunmow – Lukin went on to produce the first 'unsinkable' purpose-built lifeboat, one so light that it would hold many people safely and was also self-righting.

The Doctor's Pond at Great Dunmow was put to good use by the inventor of the lifeboat.

Lukin took his boat – the full-size version – to Trinity House to be tested. It crossed the Channel several times. However, it is said the pilot who was supposed to be testing it decided to use it for another purpose – smuggling. It is believed Lukin's boat was seized and eventually destroyed.

Undeterred, Lukin built another. This time it was taken to Bamburgh in Northumberland in 1786, where a lifeboat station had been established.

Even now Lukin is not always credited as being the inventor of the lifeboat. Claims have been made for others. There is a small plaque beside the Doctor's Pond that recognises the achievement of this perhaps otherwise unsung hero of Great Dunmow. Through his efforts, many lives have been saved.

One should just add that Lukin risked more than having his pride dented when he went to the Doctor's Pond to test his boats. Mystery surrounds the name of the pond that now has a place in maritime history, but one theory is that the local doctors kept their supply of leeches in it. One can only hope that Mr Lukin did not have to roll up the legs of his trousers and wade into the water to right his boats too often!

⁂ GREAT HALLINGBURY ⁂

The man who foiled the Gunpowder Plot
Lying at rest in the parish church at Great Hallingbury is a man who changed the course of history.

Few know that without the prompt action of William Parker, better known as Baron Monteagle, the people of Britain would not be burning effigies of Guy Fawkes every November. For Monteagle is the man credited with revealing the Gunpowder Plot in 1605.

Monteagle was himself once a Catholic, just like the conspirators he helped to thwart. He had even – like Robert Catesby, the leader of the Gunpowder Plot – involved himself in the rebellion of the Earl of Essex at the start of the seventeenth century. That earned him a spell behind bars, but, on his release, Monteagle renounced his Catholicism and wrote to James I to ask if he could be

A now almost-forgotten Essex resident was responsible for thwarting the Gunpowder Plot.

admitted to the Church of England. He was to become a great friend of the monarch – to the extent that he probably ended up saving his life.

Monteagle was among those due to sit in Parliament on 5 November 1605. One of the chief conspirators was a man named Francis Tresham, who just happened to be the brother-in-law of Monteagle. Family ties were strong and Tresham urged Catesby to spare the life of Monteagle. However, his leader refused to give him permission to warn his relative of what was in store for Parliament.

Monteagle was hosting a dinner party when a mysterious note was brought to him. The anonymous letter – possibly written by Tresham or his sister – warned Monteagle not to attend Parliament 'for God and man hath concurred to punish the wickedness of this time'. It urged him to retire to the country for his own safety, 'for though there be no appearance of any stir, yet I say they shall receive a terrible blow this Parliament, and they shall not see who hurts them'. There was no signature.

Loyal to James, Monteagle took the note to Whitehall and a search was made of the cellars of the Houses of Parliament. The rest, of course, is history. The fate of Guy Fawkes is known throughout the world.

As for Monteagle, he became a national hero – the man who saved the monarchy and Parliament. He was well rewarded for his troubles and saw out the rest of his days in prosperity. Monteagle died in 1622 and was laid to rest at Great Hallingbury, the Parker family seat situated close to the Hertfordshire border.

⚜ GREAT LEIGHS ⚜

The pub with spirits of a different kind

You would perhaps expect an inn alleged to be the oldest in the country to be home to more than its fair share of ghosts. And that is certainly the case at

St Anne's Castle claims to be the oldest inn in the country and reputedly one of the most haunted.

St Anne's Castle in Great Leighs, which has been serving travellers as far back as at least the twelfth century.

One inhabitant from beyond the grave who is said to have made her home in the establishment – a local witch – caused such a nuisance in the village that none other than Harry Price, the ghost-hunter famous for his investigations at Borley Rectory, was called in to sort it out.

The witch – Ann Hughes – was tried at nearby Chelmsford in 1621. She was found guilty of murder and executed. She is said to have been buried in Great Leighs, at the crossroads, as was normal during those times. A huge stone was also rolled over her grave, presumably to keep her in it. However, in the 1940s, against much local opposition, the stone was moved, as the road that ran alongside it was widened to cope with an increase in heavy traffic. Villagers feared that moving the grave of a witch would bring bad luck and, when some bones were discovered under the removed stone, they started to worry. Sure enough some strange happenings were reported in the village. Church bells were said to toll in the dead of night; chickens stopped laying eggs; and cows no longer produced milk – all the usual things that witches were blamed for in days gone by. People even reported seeing Ann in the pub itself.

It is said the weird goings-on only stopped when the stone was placed back on the grave at the suggestion of Harry Price. However, there were still subsequent sightings of Ann in the pub itself. No doubt she liked her new home a little too much and did not fancy the idea of going back to where she had come from.

❧ GREAT WALTHAM ❧

I told you so

Every great mansion should have a spooky tale that has been handed down the centuries. The impressive Langleys at Great Waltham, a village north of Chelmsford, does not disappoint.

Langleys was home to the Everards and, in the mid-seventeenth century, it was also home to a certain Miss Lee. Lady Everard brought the young lady up on behalf of her brother, Sir Charles Lee. When his wife died after giving birth to their daughter, the baby was placed into the care of her aunt. Lady Everard treated her niece as though she was her own daughter and she enjoyed a happy childhood at Langleys. When it was time for Miss Lee to fly the nest, a marriage was arranged and her future appeared to be rosy. However, that marriage did not take place. What followed was truly mind-boggling and also tragic.

One night Miss Lee woke believing there to be a candle still burning in her room. The maid assured her this was not the case. Miss Lee went back to sleep but woke again in the early hours of the morning and this time saw an old lady in her

A tragic tale emanates from the walls of Langleys.

room. It was her late mother. The visitor told her daughter that she was at peace and that they would be reunited at 12 o'clock that very day.

Miss Lee became convinced she was going to die and wasted no time in penning a letter to her father, to inform him of the strange and sad prophecy. Lady Everard called a physician and a surgeon, but they could find nothing physically or mentally wrong with her niece. She was in perfect health. No doubt the household tried to reassure the young woman that it had just been a dream. However, Miss Lee remained adamant that her end was near and called for the chaplain to say prayers with her. The household must have been completely bemused by what was going on, but, sure enough, on the stroke of 12 o'clock, poor Miss Lee is said to have sat down in a chair and died without any warning – apart from the one she received from her deceased mother in the dead of night, of course.

⚜ GREAT WARLEY ⚜

Money does not grow on trees
Nobody likes paying taxes. And John Evelyn – the famous diarist of the seventeenth century – was of the opinion that they were too high in Essex. In fact, during the Commonwealth, he regarded them to be so outrageously high compared to elsewhere, that he eventually sold his property in the county rather than have to pay them.

The now ruined Warley Place was once home to diarist John Evelyn. It was later taken over by the famous horticulturist Ellen Willmott.

Evelyn bought Warley Place and other parts of the manor of Great Warley, near Brentwood, in 1649. He purchased the estate from his wife's side of the family. It is said his relatives continued to reside at the manor house, while Evelyn lived elsewhere. However, he would have been a frequent 'guest' at Warley Place and displayed his love of gardening here. It is said he planted some Spanish or sweet chestnut trees that can still be seen today.

Warley Place later became a celebrated garden in Victorian and Edwardian times, when famous horticulturist Ellen Willmott resided here. It is now a nature reserve run by Essex Wildlife Trust.

Evelyn was a Royalist, so it is perhaps not surprising that he should be critical of Parliament's taxation policies. No doubt he was not the only landowner to complain, but the diarist decided to sell Warley Place in 1655 due to the high taxes imposed on Essex properties. He wrote in his famous diary: 'The taxes were so intolerable that they eat up the rents, etc, surcharged as that county [Essex] had been above all others during our unnatural war.'

One can only assume that the county was hit so hard because of its proximity to London. Some residents in the area today might argue that things have not changed much!

❧ GREENSTED ❧

The return of the king

The oldest wooden church in the world is tucked away in a rural spot just outside Chipping Ongar. It is a beautiful building and certainly fit for a king – even if it was a dead one.

For it was here the bones of St Edmund were reputedly housed for a night on their way from London to their final resting place at what is now Bury St Edmunds in Suffolk. The great abbey there is now in ruins, but pretty Greensted Church stands virtually unchanged from the day the remains of Edmund lay here for a night in 1013.

The story of brave Edmund is a stirring one. It is said he refused to abandon his Christian faith and paid the ultimate price. The Danes invaded the East of England in about 866, entering Suffolk a few years later. King Edmund of East Anglia was defeated and cruelly martyred. He was bound and tortured, but still refused to renounce his faith and, angered by his defiance, his captors are said to have riddled his body with arrows, before his head was severed and thrown into the bushes. Only when the Danes had dispersed did some of the surviving Saxons come out of hiding and recover the torso of their great leader. The head could not be found until a wolf directed them to it.

The precious remains of Edmund were carried to Bury St Edmunds, the town that is now named after him, but – following another Danish invasion in 1010 – they were transferred to London for safe keeping. Finally, some three years later, the remains made their final journey from the capital back to Bury St Edmunds, stopping at Greensted, then a forest sanctuary, on the way.

<h1 style="text-align: center;">*H*</h1>

✢ HADLEIGH ✢

A force to be reckoned with

There is no need to be scared of ghosts. After all, they cannot do you any physical harm, can they? Well, it seems they can if one is to believe a story that emanated from the ruins of Hadleigh Castle long ago.

It all started when Sally, a milkmaid, met a spectral woman in white among the ruins of the castle that is perched high above the Thames Estuary. The woman ordered Sally to return after dark when she would explain why she now haunted this particular spot. Sally, perhaps for obvious reasons, did not keep the date. However, the next day she happened to meet the ghost again. The woman in white was none too pleased that she had not returned during the night and is said to have given the bemused Sally a cuff round the ears. It must have been done with some force because the strike almost dislocated the milkmaid's neck and, from that day on, she was known among her friends as 'wry-neck Sal'.

The ruins of Hadleigh Castle, a perfect spot for a spooky tale.

❦ HADSTOCK ❦

A 'reeking' door hangs longest

Many who enter the parish church at Hadstock close to the Cambridgeshire border are blissfully unaware that they have done something quite remarkable.

No doubt they would have entered the building via what is said to be the oldest door in the country still in constant use.

The ancient door at St Botolph's Church is thought to date back to about 1020. If it could talk, it would be able to tell us much. In fact, it did hold a secret that only came to light in more recent times. During repair work, human skin was found under the ironwork. It would have belonged to a very unfortunate person. It was not uncommon for someone guilty of committing a sacrilegious act during the Middle Ages to be flayed alive, their skin nailed on the church door as a warning to all. If the gruesome sight had not been enough to put people off, the smell should have done the trick!

❦ HALSTEAD ❦

Going Dutch

You never know how much you will miss someone until they are gone.

That can certainly be said of the town of Halstead back in the sixteenth century. The residents did all they could to rid the town of rival Dutch weavers, but then did all they could to try to get them to come back. Sadly, it was too late by then.

Protestants primarily from the Low Countries fled to England to escape religious persecution, the majority settling in Colchester. They set themselves up as weavers and established a thriving cloth trade. More and more followed until Colchester was bursting at the seams, if you excuse the pun. So, in 1576, some of the Dutch weavers were given permission to up sticks and move to nearby Halstead. There was already a cloth trade here and it soon began to suffer with the arrival of the superior Dutch weavers. The finer cloths of the newcomers were considered to be a far better product. The locals were also bitter over the fact that the Dutch, because of their reputation for producing excellent cloth, were allowed to put a seal of quality on their own products. The Halstead weavers had to go through a process of inspection by an independent party.

It was not long before the simmering discontent reached boiling point. And when the Dutch discovered that some of the Halstead weavers had started to counterfeit their seal of excellence, they deemed that to be the last straw. The furious men of the Low Countries packed up their looms and left.

Townsford Mill is a reminder of when cloth and silk was big business in Halstead.

The locals were delighted and believed the victory was theirs. They were wrong. It appears their own products had only been selling off the reputation of those produced by their Dutch counterparts. Once their Dutch neighbours had left, demand for Halstead cloth dropped dramatically.

With no other option, the people of Halstead decided to swallow their pride and apologise to the Dutch. In doing so, they pleaded for them to return and even petitioned Queen Elizabeth to get her to order them to come back, but all to no avail.

Fortunately for the town of Halstead, business did improve in later years. George Courtauld opened his first silk mill in Braintree in 1809. The business flourished and another mill was established at Halstead. It is said that Townsford Mill, which still stands in the town, employed more than 1,000 people by the mid-nineteenth century. It was from Halstead that silk was produced to make mourning gowns for Queen Victoria.

✤ HANNINGFIELD RESERVOIR ✤

What lies beneath
Amid the cries and shrieks of migrating wildfowl at Hanningfield Reservoir near Chelmsford, you might just make out the sound of church bells.

Some say there is a lost village submerged in the dark waters of Hanningfield Reservoir.

However, if you were to answer their call to attend evensong you would need to swap your Sunday best for a diving suit. For these bells, according to local folklore, belong to a church submerged in the dark waters of the reservoir. For many years after the Sandon Valley was flooded, rumours abounded that some buildings remained intact deep below the surface. And some claimed they could even hear the distant sound of the church bells ringing from deep below.

It is not an old legend. Hanningfield Reservoir – the second largest in Essex after Abberton near Colchester – was only created in the 1950s. It is now home to a popular nature reserve.

The idea of there being a lost village under the water is a charming one, but sadly it does not really have any foundation. All the buildings were supposedly demolished before the area was flooded. The once grand sixteenth-century manor house called Fremnells was among them. That building itself held many secrets. It is reputed to have had a mysterious room that Dick Turpin and Black Bess used as a hiding place. It is said that stone from the walls of what was the area's grandest house was used to provide the foundation of the reservoir's dams.

✢ HARWICH ✢

The misleading lights

Not many places could claim to have had two working lighthouses, but there was a time when not even two could prevent vessels from coming a cropper at Harwich.

In fact, in their finals days, those two beacons were actually the cause of mariners coming to grief.

They were dubbed the 'misleading lights' of Harwich and finally became redundant in 1863, though, it has to be said, through no fault of their own. The Low Lighthouse and High Lighthouse, which still stand, were in perfect working order mechanically when their lights were switched off for the final time. They were built in 1818 to guide ships safely into the famous seaport, and, by all accounts, they did a good job. When brought into line, they showed ships a safe channel into the harbour. The two lights in alignment told the skipper when it was safe to turn into the mouth of the harbour. In fact, they were so successful that the owner became very wealthy by charging a penny per ton light dues on all cargoes coming into the port.

Trinity House acquired the lighthouses in 1836, but their days were numbered due to silting, which gradually changed the course of the channel. Only through

The Low Lighthouse and its 'sibling', the High Lighthouse, in the distance.

experience did unwary mariners start to realise that the lights were now useless and actually responsible for misleading them.

The Low Lighthouse is now a museum and, along with its 'sibling', a prominent local landmark.

⚜ HATFIELD PEVEREL ⚜

Don't bare your soul

If the Devil himself vows he will have your soul whether you are buried inside or outside a church, you have a problem. There appears to be no safe resting place away from his clutches.

However, Ingelrica came up with a solution. On her death in about 1100 she was reputedly buried neither inside nor outside, but within the wall of the parish church at Hatfield Peverel, near Witham.

Ingelrica was well aware of her past sins and obviously very fearful for the future of her soul. The odd solution to the problem was, in fact, not a unique one. There are other tales of people requesting to be buried neither inside nor outside a church, but halfway in and halfway out in a bid to fool Old Nick.

Ingelrica was the one-time mistress of William the Conqueror and bore him a son, also named William. When the elder William tired of Ingelrica he married her off to one of his knights, Ranulph Peverel, whose estates included Hadfelda, his name later added to form what we now know as Hatfield Peverel.

Ingelrica is said to have felt guilty for her past transgressions and tried to make amends by founding a religious college in the village. Her son William turned it into a priory following his mother's death, but only the current parish church now remains, and even that has changed much since Ingelrica was reputedly laid to rest here. Needless to say, Ingelrica still did not think her later charitable acts had been enough to atone for her sins, and went for her unusual burial as a little extra insurance.

Ingelrica is said to have been buried within the wall of the parish church at Hatfield Peverel.

❧ HEMPSTEAD ❧

Heroes and villains

It is sad – but perhaps no surprise – that most people come to Hempstead because of a notorious villain and are oblivious to the fact that a national hero lies at rest here.

Highwayman Dick Turpin – born at Hempstead at the beginning of the eighteenth century – is responsible for luring most sightseers to this rural spot not too far from Saffron Walden. And most leave still none the wiser as to the far worthier achievements of William Harvey. This now almost-forgotten man was responsible for one of the greatest medical discoveries of all time. He was the first to discover the circulation of blood. That might not seem so remarkable in this day and age – it is something we now take for granted – but in the seventeenth century it was an outrageous idea.

Harvey was a humble and gentle man, a far cry from the villainous Turpin, who was born some 150 years after Harvey was laid to rest here. The physician shied away from fame and fortune, and it is said he did not make his discovery public for some twelve years. Harvey knew it would cause a stir among medical and scientific circles. It did. Many thought he was mad to suggest such an idea. Nobody before Harvey had put forward the theory that blood moved throughout the body in a continuous stream, or concluded that the heart was a muscle responsible for the process.

It is said that Harvey was not bothered by what people thought about his theory. He just wanted to discover the truth. While many at first ridiculed him, the wiser amongst them did not take long to realise he was right. The treatise in which he published his findings in 1628 is now regarded as one of the most important medical books of all time. As treatments improved thanks to his discovery, the fame of Harvey grew. However, he was never happier than when he had his head in a book. There is a charming story from the Civil War when Harvey, forever the scholar, was doing just that at almost the cost of his life and those of the royal princes in his charge. As he was the physician to Charles I, the monarch entrusted sons Charles and James to the care of Harvey during the Battle of Edgehill. Seemingly not interested in the raging conflict, Harvey is said to have withdrawn under a tree and coolly taken out his pocket book in anticipation of further study. As he had his head in a book – the princes no doubt left to amuse themselves – a cannon ball landed just a few feet from the party, forcing the scholar and his charges to make a hasty retreat.

Harvey at least has a fitting memorial in the parish church at Hempstead, even if few make a pilgrimage to view it. If they did, they would also find the memorial to another Harvey that was famous in his day. Admiral Sir Eliab Harvey, also buried in the church, was one of Lord Nelson's bravest officers. He commanded the *Temeraire*, the ship made famous by the painting of Turner. It is said that when

Nelson lay dying during the Battle of Trafalgar, soldiers from the French ship *Redoutable* managed to board the *Victory*, and it was only the intervention of the *Temeraire* that saved it.

Sir Eliab was a hero, but he could be a little villainous at times. He was famously dismissed from the navy at one point for daring to question why another had been chosen for a top position ahead of him. Fortunately, it is for his heroism that he is better remembered these days, though, like William Harvey, he will always have to live in the shadow of another in the village of Hempstead.

Return to sender: Dick Turpin

The true identity of Dick Turpin might never have come to light if a relative had not refused to pay the cost of a stamp.

And a man named 'John Palmer' would have been hanged in York with probably very little fuss. That man Palmer was none other than the notorious highwayman himself. Turpin was forced to flee Epping Forest, the scene of most of his crimes, and start a new life in the north of the country. He eventually settled in Yorkshire and, under the assumed name John Palmer, took on the guise of a gentleman horse dealer. Turpin is said to have certainly dealt in horses, but, unbeknown to the fellow gentlemen he now called his friends, he stole their trusted steeds from almost under their noses. It is said that he would steal a horse from a particular gentleman and then have the nerve to sell it back to him, the buyer oblivious to the fact that he was buying his own horse. Those particular crimes only came to light because of a far more trivial offence. Turpin was arrested after threatening a labourer who had taken offence to him wantonly shooting a fowl.

As he awaited his fate in jail, the authorities were still oblivious to his true identity. He might have gone to the gallows as a horse stealer called John Palmer, his execution no different to the many others of the time. No one had any idea that he was Dick Turpin – the most wanted man in England.

Turpin only received the send-off he perhaps deserved when, in desperation, he wrote from jail to his brother-in-law at Hempstead, the village where Turpin was born. That letter was returned to the post office unopened. It is not clear why his relative did not pay the delivery charge. However, it was to change the course of history. It is said the letter somehow came into the hands of a schoolmaster who had taught Turpin to write as a child back in Hempstead. He recognised the writing and, when the letter was opened, all finally put two and two together, and realised that John Palmer was none other than Dick Turpin.

It meant that the execution of perhaps England's most infamous villain became a far bigger affair than it would have been; and if it had not been for a 'stingy' relative and sharp-eyed schoolmaster, the legend of Dick Turpin would have had a very different ending.

⚜ HEYBRIDGE ⚜

The writer full of hot air

Nineteenth-century printer and writer Charles Clark found a novel way to reduce his distribution costs.

In the days before email, it was not easy to reach a wide audience when you had something to say. Clark, who penned curious verses and satires, would sometimes attach his compositions to balloons. If there was a decent wind, his words of wisdom might have reached people in faraway places.

Those lucky enough to catch a balloon to read one of his ditties could have been forgiven for being slightly perplexed. Clark was particularly fond of acrostics and occasionally produced verses that rhymed not only at the end of the line, but also at the beginning. He was also fond of puns.

Clark was born at Heybridge, near Maldon, and retired to the village of his birth, living at Great Totham in between, where he was affectionately known as the 'Bard of Totham'. He was considered something of an eccentric among his neighbours.

Clark owned his own printing press, which was handy, as one wonders how many publishers would have deemed his work worthy to make it into print. Among his contributions to English literature was a new version of

Look out for some balloons in the sky at Heybridge Basin.

the national anthem entitled 'God Stop the Queen'. Clark, a supporter of birth control, believed the population was growing too fast and suggested the queen herself should set an example by stopping producing children. It is not thought that his anthem took off – apart from when it was attached to a few balloons, of course!

❖ HIGH BEACH ❖

The doctor and two 'mad' poets

Matthew Allen was a doctor who made one 'mad' poet sane and another sane poet 'mad'.

Dr Allen set up a private lunatic asylum at High Beach in the heart of Epping Forest. Among his patients was melancholy scribe John Clare. He was in Dr Allen's care from 1837–41. Clare was to benefit from the doctor's pioneering approach to insanity. Asylums of the past were often inhumane and cruel places. Dr Allen did much to change this. His patients were treated as human beings and his work brought him much attention, not only within medical circles, but within the literary world too. One of the doctor's neighbours was Alfred Lord Tennyson and he stayed as a guest at Dr Allen's asylum for a couple of weeks. Tennyson was himself not always in the best of spirits during the three years he lived at High Beach. He came to Essex in 1837, leaving his sweetheart Emily Sellwood back in Lincolnshire. He claimed he did not even have enough money to pay the fare to visit her. At times Tennyson became very depressed by the whole situation, so it is perhaps no wonder that, following his visit to Dr Allen's institution, he declared that the 'mad people' were 'the most agreeable and most reasonable persons' he had met. Certainly, Dr Allen's methods appeared to help Clare. The doctor believed Epping Forest was the perfect location for his establishment, his patients able to benefit from the fresh air and secluded walks among the trees that were good for both body and mind. Clare improved enough to pen some of his poems at the asylum, which was established within three properties in Lippitts Hill. He also seemingly recovered well enough to discharge himself, walking all the way back to his home in Northamptonshire. However, it appears his recovery was only temporary, as later that year he was certified insane and moved to a county asylum.

If Dr Allen can gain some credit in helping to make Clare sane, at least for a temporary period, he must also be blamed for making Tennyson 'mad' – at least hopping mad! Tennyson, in later years, was certainly to regret his acquaintance with the doctor. Not long after Clare had left the asylum, Dr Allen set up a company for carving wood by machine. It is said he convinced Tennyson, who had by then left Essex, to invest the money he had now acquired through his poetry in the project. However, the enterprise failed and Dr Allen eventually became bankrupt in 1843. Poor Tennyson also lost everything in the venture and that, no doubt, would have blackened his memory of Essex even more.

It was not all doom and gloom during his spell at Beech Hill House, however. Tennyson wrote part of his famous epic *In Memoriam* here. He did enjoy the forest and went on long walks. During the winter he could be seen skating on the frozen pond. On hearing the bells of nearby Waltham Abbey during one festive period, it is said he penned the famous line: 'Ring out the old, ring in the new.'

❦ HIGH LAVER ❦

The guest who stayed for more than thirteen years
It is unlikely that the great philosopher John Locke would have needed references when he became a lodger at the once lavish house of Oates in the village of High Laver.

At the time, he was recognised as the most brilliant man of his age and everyone was talking about him.

For that reason, it is perhaps a little curious that a man whose work made him the centre of attention should remove himself from the spotlight and live the rest of his life in rural seclusion. Life at High Laver, near Harlow, could not have been a bigger contrast to life in the capital. Anybody who was anybody usually made their base in London. It was the place to be, where the great minds would spend many hours discussing their philosophies.

It is said Locke first came to Oates, the home of his good friends the Mashams, for health reasons. He suffered from chronic asthma and this was perhaps a good enough reason to conclude that the fresh country air would be more beneficial than the smoke of London. Some have even suggested he was tired of being the centre of attention and craved the quiet life.

Locke was first invited to Oates as a guest of the Mashams. However, he ended up staying more than thirteen years. It is not thought that Locke outstayed his welcome. It was Lady Masham herself who suggested he should lodge with the family on a permanent basis. Like Locke, Lady Masham was an intellectual and the two got on splendidly. They would spend many an evening discussing politics and religion, ensuring the philosopher did not miss the stimulating conversation of his fellow thinkers who he had left behind in the capital. Sir Francis Masham was a man of the country who was presumably happy to let Locke and his wife get on with putting the world to rights.

It is said Locke paid £1 a week for his board and lodging, which included menservants. He was given an apartment, consisting of a bedroom and study,

Philosopher John Locke is buried at sleepy High Laver and not with his peers in the capital.

but lived with the family most of the time. He would certainly have needed more than a bedsit, as Locke had a personal library of some 4,000 books. Most landlords might have cringed to see the new lodger bringing so many suitcases up the garden path, but the scholarly Lady Masham was probably licking her lips in anticipation.

At first Locke travelled to London on a regular basis, but as the years went on he withdrew even further into his rural existence. Friends and colleagues had to come to see him. Isaac Newton was among the high-profile guests at Oates.

While many would have questioned whether High Laver was the right place for the greatest intellectual of the day, others might have said it was the perfect place, the peace and quiet giving him much time to think. And think he did, as well as write; Locke continued to produce some great works while living at Oates.

The fact that Locke did not return to London and was happy to spend the rest of his life in someone else's house suggests that he was satisfied with his lot in life. His epitaph, which he himself wrote, provides further evidence. Locke, who died in 1704 with Lady Masham reading to him from the Book of Psalms, wrote: 'If you ask what manner of man he was, he answers that he lived content with his own fortune.'

That might also go some way to explaining why the great John Locke now lies buried in the churchyard at High Laver and not in London with his intellectual peers.

❖ HUTTON ❖

A policeman's lot is not a happy one

Few drivers on the main road from Billericay to Brentwood notice a small stone memorial on the grass verge at Hutton. And, because it is a road that sees few pedestrians willing to brave it, not many will have read the inscription. In fact, many Hutton residents do not even know of its existence.

It was on this same road that PC Robert Bamborough walked with a prisoner in 1850. The memorial now marks the spot somewhere nearby where he became the first Essex police officer to be killed on duty.

In those days there was little passing traffic and few would have even noticed the policeman and the man handcuffed to him.

The roadside memorial to an unfortunate policeman.

PC Bamborough was escorting convicted poacher William Wood from Billericay to Brentwood. On reaching a particularly isolated spot, Wood made his bid for freedom, but it came at a huge cost. Still bound together, the two tussled and fell into a nearby pond. Wood managed to free himself and made a run for it. However, he must have been feeling some pangs of guilt, for, before he was out of sight, Wood returned to the pond and lifted the head of the injured PC Bamborough out of the water. He then fled the scene. It may have been a remote spot, but his one act of mercy just happened to be witnessed by a third party. When Wood was later caught and went to trial, he was spared the death penalty for murder, the evidence of that witness backing up his claim that he did not purposely kill Bamborough. Instead, Wood was sentenced to life transportation for manslaughter.

Sadly, PC Bamborough never recovered from his injuries and died a few days after the incident. The brave policeman earned the unenviable distinction of becoming – just ten years after Essex Police was founded – the first officer killed in the line of duty. Sadly, he was not to be the last.

J

❧ INGATESTONE ❧

'Judas' and the priest

Every stately home should have a secret room.

Ingatestone Hall does not disappoint. The impressive house has not one, but two. Of course, they are no longer secret and are what many paying visitors to the house come to see these days. That would not have been the case in Elizabethan times.

The priest holes were a necessity and it was vital they remained a secret during what were troubled times for practising Catholics.

Ingatestone Hall had many secrets.

The term priest hole is given to any hiding place for priests. Most of the principal Catholic homes had at least one. Ingatestone Hall was the home of the Petres during the reign of Queen Elizabeth, a prominent and influential family with Catholic sympathies.

Lady Petre was a devout papist and, following the death of her husband Sir William, harboured many seminary priests. Secret services were regularly held at her home, though it was a risky business.

The most famous Catholic to find shelter within the walls of Ingatestone Hall was John Payne. He resided here in the guise of an estate steward. The priest holes were not enough to protect him, however, and he became the only Catholic priest to be executed in Essex during the reign of Elizabeth. He was actually betrayed by a man who served under the same roof at Ingatestone. George 'Judas' Eliot – as he is known within Catholic circles – was an apostate Catholic who became a spy. He was a servant at Ingatestone Hall when Payne was here. Eliot went on to betray Payne and gave evidence against him at his trial. Eliot, despite being under oath, claimed that Payne had uttered treasonable words against the queen while residing at Ingatestone. It is generally accepted that Payne was innocent of the charges. He had no desire to help more rebellious Catholics in their attempts to unseat Elizabeth and restore Catholicism as the national religion. He only wanted to be allowed to worship in the way he pleased. Payne, who was canonised by the Roman Catholic Church in 1970, was tortured before his execution in 1582. He was condemned to die as a traitor, to be hanged, drawn and quartered. However, he was so loved by the people that they appealed to the hangman to ensure he was dead before cutting him down to at least spare him any further agony.

What mighty contests rise from trivial things

You would presume that someone as vain as Robert Petre would have thought twice about cutting the hair of his sweetheart for a prank.

He probably regretted it at any rate.

Beautiful Arabella Fermor was said to be horrified when she discovered he had snipped off a lock of her hair during a party in 1711. Her family were none too pleased either and it led to a major feud between both families, which one of the greatest writers of the age tried to settle by making light of the situation. As Alexander Pope wrote in his celebrated poem 'The Rape of the Lock': 'What mighty contests rise from trivial things.'

No doubt the impudent and rash Lord Petre believed the incident to be trivial, but he certainly would not have liked anyone doing the same to him. Petre is said to have chosen not to wear the standard wig of the day, preferring to spend up to six hours a day dressing his own hair.

Arabella was a distant cousin of Petre, the Petre family home being the famous Ingatestone Hall. His joke certainly backfired. The two lovers –

though some claim it was merely a romantic dalliance – never went on to wed, even though the families are believed to have eventually shaken hands. That they did was probably due to Pope. A friend of both the Fermors and Petres suggested to his friend Pope that the poet penned one of his humorous verses, in the hope that comedy would defuse the situation. The aim was to 'laugh at the two [families] together'. The result was 'The Rape of the Lock', published in 1712. However, the first edition of the satire is said to have enraged the Petres even further, as they believed that Arabella, in being portrayed as a heroine, became a little too big for her boots following publication. However, it appears 'The Rape of the Lock' did serve its purpose in getting all involved to eventually realise that the whole incident had been blown out of proportion.

One who certainly was left laughing – apart from his readers – was Pope himself, as his poem proved to be a massive success.

❧ KELVEDON ❧

The Prince of Preachers

Churches that struggle to fill their pews these days could do with someone like Charles Haddon Spurgeon.

It is said there was no building big enough to hold the amount of people that wanted to listen to this remarkable preacher. In the end one had to be built specially for him, and even that proved inadequate.

Spurgeon – who was born at Kelvedon, near Witham, in 1834 – was a Nonconformist. By the time he was eighteen, he was already a Baptist pastor. Spurgeon was still only twenty when he was called to serve New Park Street Chapel in Southwark (later the Metropolitan Tabernacle), which already had the largest Baptist congregation in London at the time.

Within a year, the chapel he served had to be enlarged, but, as work was being carried out, it soon became obvious that even the new home for his ever-increasing congregation would not be large enough. All the capital – and soon the country – was talking about this brilliant young orator. People flocked from all over to hear him preach. Eventually, in 1861, a tabernacle had to be built to hold his services. It could house some 6,000 people and was packed each time Spurgeon was in the pulpit until his death in 1892. His sermons were printed and sold for a penny. People bought them as though it was their newspaper. Soon the sermons of this son of Kelvedon went all over the world. It is said that more than 50 million copies were printed and circulated as far as Australia and the United States. That figure did not even include the many that appeared in newspapers and other publications.

Even though Spurgeon was a Nonconformist, he reached all denominations. High Anglicans and even Roman Catholics wanted to know what he had to say. Spurgeon had the world waiting with bated breath for his next sermon.

It is therefore perhaps strange that so few Kelvedon residents are aware that Spurgeon, who could only be described as a megastar of his time, was born in their village. Most who walk past his birthplace do not even notice the blue plaque dedicated to his memory that is positioned high on the wall of the cottage.

The Kelvedon birthplace of a man that churches would love in their pulpits today.

It is also perhaps a little curious that Spurgeon – still referred to as the 'Prince of Preachers' – is believed to have never returned to Kelvedon as an adult. He was invited to preach here on at least one occasion, but declined the offer for some unknown reason. It is a little sad that the village never personally got the chance to welcome 'home' its most famous son or to hear, within its own walls, those words of wisdom that once reached audiences throughout the world.

An ordinary bungalow in Kelvedon Hatch?

⁘ KELVEDON HATCH ⁘

The bungalow that was made as safe as houses
Standing just off the busy A128, between Brentwood and Chipping Ongar at Kelvedon Hatch, is a bungalow.

It looks like most bungalows built during the 1950s.

And that is the point. It was meant to look like most bungalows in the 1950s.

However, this particular bungalow was built to hide a quite incredible secret – one that was only revealed some forty years later. For, some 100ft beneath this bungalow was – and still is – a nuclear bunker.

During the Cold War, a local farmer called Parrish received a visit from the War Office. He was told that 25 acres of his land was being requisitioned. Locals must have wondered what on earth was going on when the designated area was sealed off. The roads were closed and armed guards patrolled the site. There was strictly no public access.

Nobody was told what was going on beyond the high fences. Even most of those involved in the construction of the bunker – made to sign the Official Secrets Act – were oblivious to what the end result would be. Builders had their own job to do and would have had no idea what other builders were doing.

People must have wondered what all the fuss was about when building work was completed in 1953. All that was visible on the surface was a bungalow, which was really the entrance to a labyrinth of rooms deep below.

The bunker was built to house up to 600 military and civilian personnel, including the prime minister. Had there been a nuclear attack, it was from here the government would have organised the survivors in the outside world, thanks to the bunker's own radio studio. The occupants of the bunker, protected by 10ft-thick reinforced concrete walls, could have survived in their underground world for up to three months. It had its own water supply and electricity generators. It is said that a staggering 40 tons of concrete was used in constructing the bunker.

With the ending of the Cold War, the bunker soon became redundant. It was eventually decommissioned in the early 1990s. The Parrish family got their land back but decided to open the bunker to the public. It means that Kelvedon Hatch Secret Nuclear Bunker is now an unusual tourist attraction and, it goes without saying, is no longer a secret!

Everybody needs good neighbours
Disputes between neighbours are not uncommon.

However, few can have gone to the extent that one resident of Kelvedon Hatch went to in order to pay back a neighbour who had riled him.

It could not have been a spur of the moment act of revenge either, as it involved the individual getting in the builders. And their handiwork still stands on the main Brentwood to Chipping Ongar road, a visible reminder of a feud that probably went a little bit too far.

Brizes, now home to a private school, is an impressive mansion even today. It was once called Bryce and was the home of the Royds family. In 1906, Mr Royds decided to bring charges against a neighbour who had shot a pheasant on his land. That particular neighbour was fined in court and was so incensed that the matter had been taken that far, that he vowed to get his revenge. Knowing he could not trespass on their land for fear of finding himself in court again, he had to come up with another plan, one that he knew would irk his neighbour. He decided he needed to do something that would remind the Roydses of their actions every single day of their lives. The view from Bryce was an unbroken one and so the vindictive neighbour decided he would create a blot on the landscape. He ordered for a row of cottages to be built on his land – in full view of his neighbour's home.

The cottages still stand and locals now refer to them as the IOU cottages.

There is another stately home in Kelvedon Hatch that is worth a mention. Kelvedon Hall was home to the Wrights. One of the Wrights moved to the United States and became an ancestor of the famous Wright brothers, pioneers of the aeroplane.

⚜ LAYER MARNEY ⚜

Marney's ghost

If you want something done properly, you best do it yourself.

Unfortunately for Sir Henry Marney, he had to rely on his son to finish the job of supervising the construction of Layer Marney Tower.

Lord Marney, the elder, died in 1523 before his great project was completed. It was left to his son, the 2nd Lord Marney, to finish it. Those who visit what is now the tallest surviving Tudor gatehouse in England cannot see much wrong with it, but the original Lord Marney did not appear to be very happy with the way it was finished. It was not to his liking. And that is the reason why the furious ghost of Lord Marney has been spotted on a number of occasions hurtling up and down the stairs of the tower.

Layer Marney Tower is reputedly still home to its creator.

Lord Marney, the elder, was an important figure in royal circles and the friend of many kings. He held various top positions under Henry VIII. He was made a baron shortly before his death and wanted to build a home worthy of a man of his status. Having been buried in the church that stands in the shadow of his great tower, Sir Henry was at close hand to ensure his son finished the project in a satisfactory manner. It appears he did not.

⁂ LITTLE BADDOW ⁂

Taking the biscuit

Hansel and Gretel were to rue the birds that ate the crumbs they had left to form a trail.

However, some thieves that struck a Little Baddow pub in 1842 must have wished there had been some feathered friends to eat the remains of their impromptu repast. The trail of biscuit crumbs they inadvertently left behind led to their capture.

The men had raided the old Rodney inn, which was situated a little further along from the present Rodney pub.

It was after hours when they broke in, and the occupants of the pub, all women, had retired for the night. The raiders threatened them as they lay in their beds, and demanded money. The frightened women told them that there was some cash in the bar and that they could help themselves. And that is what they most certainly did. It is said they were in the bar for more than an hour. No doubt they also helped themselves to plenty of ale and left the establishment a little worse for wear. It appears they gorged themselves on plenty of biscuits too, as on the following morning, a sharp-eyed policeman – on being told that some biscuits were among the items that had been taken – noticed some crumbs on the lane that led to Danbury. The game was afoot. The constable was in no doubt that the gang had gone off in that direction. When he reached the village, a witness informed him that some drunken yobs had been seen heading towards Maldon. Hot on the trail, the policeman finally caught up with some drunks in a pub at Hazeleigh. He was sure they were his men, and became even more convinced when he felt in their pockets and found more crumbs from the biscuits that had led this very shrewd constable to their exact whereabouts.

Poor Alice took drastic steps

Take a stroll along an avenue of trees from the splendid house of Great Graces at Little Baddow towards Sandon Brook and you will be following in the footsteps of Lady Alice Mildmay.

She would have done this walk on numerous occasions in the first half of the seventeenth century. And it is said she still does it now.

Alice was the wife of Sir Henry Mildmay. It is said he treated her cruelly and, one day in 1615, she left the house and walked down Graces Walk, as it is now known, passing those same trees that she had passed on numerous other occasions. However, this time she did not return. When she reached Sandon Brook she drowned herself.

The path Alice took remains open to the public and, on an overcast day, with the wind blowing through the leaves of the tall trees flanking it, it is not difficult to imagine a forlorn figure heading off into the distance.

Some say Alice Mildmay still walks the lonely path from Great Graces to Sandon Brook.

⁖ LITTLE CANFIELD ⁖

Long live the Wyatts

There must be something in the air at Little Canfield, near Great Dunmow.

It certainly appears to be a good place to reside if you want to live to a grand age.

The Wyatt family are testament to that. Many members of the family who now lie at the parish church defied the odds to live long lives at a time when octogenarians, nonagenarians and centenarians were a rarity.

And if Richard Wyatt, who died in 1664 after reaching his century is anything to go by, they were a sprightly lot even in their latter days. It is said he walked from his Little Canfield home to Thavies Inn in London in a single day. In those times that was perhaps not that unusual, but Wyatt was ninety-nine at the time!

Not to be outdone, his son – also called Richard – himself clocked up a century of years.

⚜ LITTLE DUNMOW ⚜

Bringing home the bacon

Some might say that couples who don't have a single argument for a year and a day deserve more than a side of bacon. However, that was – and still is – the prize on offer to those who can prove they live in marital bliss.

The origin of what is probably the most famous Essex custom is something of a mystery. Most credit Robert Fitzwalter – leader of the rebel barons who forced King John to seal the Magna Carta in 1215 – as being the initiator of the Dunmow Flitch Trials. It is said that a year and a day after their marriage, Mr and Mrs Fitzwalter, the lord

and lady of the manor of Little Dunmow, sought a blessing from the Church. The prior who conducted the blessing was so impressed by their love and devotion that he gave them a flitch (a side of bacon). The Fitzwalters were dressed in humble clothes, disguised as peasants, which meant that the holy man was unaware of their true identity. A side of bacon would have been a valuable gift to the average labourer and his family. In return, it is said Fitzwalter gave some of his land to the priory on condition that a flitch be presented annually to any couple who could prove they had not had a cross word or regretted their marriage for one whole year and a day.

A side of bacon at Little Dunmow forms one of the more unusual inn signs in England.

The custom is still going strong, though the Flitch Trials now take place only every leap year and in neighbouring Great Dunmow. Couples have to convince a mock court of their devotion for each other, and, those who do, still receive a side of bacon as their reward.

⚜ LITTLE EASTON ⚜

Don't monkey around with fire

If they had caught the culprit responsible for setting light to Easton Lodge in 1918 it is very likely he or she would have been forgiven.

The eccentric owner of the house in Little Easton, near Great Dunmow, would probably have given them a big cuddle – and perhaps a juicy banana if they were lucky.

For the 'arsonist' is said to have been none other than a pet monkey.

The Countess of Warwick – a famous socialite – lived with lots of animals that were given a free run of the house and grounds. She was a lifelong protector of wildlife and treated her pets as though they were her children. It is said the monkey fell sick and was recovering in the house. It was left alone one night with a blanket and a roaring coal fire. That proved to be not a very good combination. It is assumed the monkey got out of its bed (perhaps to stoke the fire) and inadvertently let the flames lick the dangling blanket. It became a burning torch and presumably the terrified monkey, rather than letting go of it, started to run about the house in utter panic, spreading the blaze as it did. Of course, one will never know what really happened and it is not even known what happened to the poor monkey. What is known is that the Countess did not lose her love for animals. In fact, nearing the end of her life, she offered her estate to London Zoo, but that particular organisation declined the offer, as it had just acquired land at Whipsnade in the Chilterns for its new wildlife park.

The Countess of Warwick, *née* Frances Evelyn Maynard, inherited Easton Lodge as a toddler. She grew up to be a society beauty. She led a life of extravagance and became famous for her many affairs, none more notable than with Edward, Prince of Wales, who later became Edward VII. He called her his 'Darling Daisy', their love for each other becoming the inspiration for the music hall song *Daisy Bell*, with its immortal line, 'Daisy, Daisy, give me your answer do, I'm half crazy all for the love of you'.

Easton Lodge was the venue for lavish gatherings and entertainments. Anyone who was anyone would be in attendance. The Countess famously converted a tithe barn on the estate into a theatre. The top stars of the day, including Dame Ellen Terry, performed here. Writer H.G. Wells had a house on the estate for a spell and was a close friend of the Countess.

In later life, 'Darling Daisy' turned her back on her glamorous lifestyle and became a socialist. Her outlook on life became very different. Rather than be the

Easton Lodge and its beautiful gardens was once home to an eccentric countess and her many animals.

centre of attention among the leading lights of the day, the Countess of Warwick became content to live a quiet life surrounded by her beloved animals.

The gardens of Easton Lodge are occasionally open to the public. You can still see the odd peacock in the beautiful grounds, strutting in the shadow of what is left of the once grand house. Sadly, you are unlikely to encounter any monkeys these days.

⊹ LITTLE HALLINGBURY ⊹

'Chart' a different course

The village of Little Hallingbury, situated close to the Hertfordshire border, might have been very different than it is today.

Few outside of the parish know that it just missed out on being home to what is now the world-famous Charterhouse School.

Thomas Sutton, founder of the establishment, had chosen Little Hallingbury to be the site of a hospital for pensioners and a school for some forty boys. It made sense at the time. Sutton owned a number of manors close to Saffron Walden and knew the area well. It was 1611 and he was nearing the end of a successful life. He wanted to do some good for those he was soon to leave behind. It is said that Sutton made his fortune by the discovery of coal on two of his estates near Newcastle and was reputed to be the richest commoner of the time.

It is not known how far down the line the project to found a school had gone, but, by all accounts, it was at a very late stage when the proposed location was switched from Little Hallingbury to Smithfield, on a site of a former great religious house.

Charterhouse, one of the top public schools in the country, is now based at Godalming, Surrey. However, it still has links with Little Hallingbury. Part of the parish churchyard is owned by the establishment and is still used for the burial of Charterhouse Brothers.

❧ LITTLE MAPLESTEAD ❧

The shape of things that have been

Little Maplestead is a long way from Jerusalem. And yet there is a link between the two places – one that is still visible through the remarkable church found in this part of rural Essex.

The parish church at Little Maplestead, near Halstead, is one of only a few round churches in England that still stands. The fact it is of that shape is evidence that the manor was once in the hands of the Order of the Knights Hospitaller. The religious order was founded in the Holy Land in the eleventh century to offer medical care to the sick and injured Crusaders. It was granted land throughout Europe, Little Maplestead coming into its hands in about 1185. The monks built churches that were modelled on the fourth-century rotunda Church of the Holy Sepulchre at Jerusalem, one of the most distinctive buildings in the world, erected on the supposed site of the tomb of Christ.

The current church at Little Maplestead only dates back to the fourteenth century, but most believe it was built on the site of the original church that was here two centuries earlier. The building of round churches had actually gone out of fashion by then, so it is something of a mystery why the replacement one at Little Maplestead should also have been built to that shape. One can only assume that the knights were fond of the original design and decided to copy it. Like the knights themselves, the church is dedicated to St John the Baptist.

After the demise of the Knights Templar – another famous order of warrior monks – the Hospitallers were granted much of the land that once belonged to their rivals. The Hospitallers existed as a religious order until Henry VIII dissolved the monasteries. However, the church at Little Maplestead survived and has probably changed very little since the knights worshipped in it.

Like the Templars, the Hospitallers combined the religious life of a monk with the fighting life of a knight. However, the Order never forgot its original aim in caring for the sick and injured. Indeed, the dress of the knights would be familiar to us today. On their black mantles was an eight-pointed white cross, the emblem still used by the St John Ambulance service, one of the organisations that originated from this once very powerful religious order.

The church at Little Maplestead is one of only a few round churches still standing in England.

⚜ LITTLE WIGBOROUGH ⚜

Airships that pass in the night

It is usually recorded that there were no casualties when a German Zeppelin was forced to land in the remote village of Little Wigborough, near Mersea Island, during the First World War. Sadly, that is not strictly true.

There is a gravestone in the churchyard that records one casualty of that fateful night in September 1916.

Alfred Wright had, like many, not failed to notice the ball of fire as the German crew – all of whom had survived the impact – set their airship alight after being forced to land at New Hall Farm. He got on his motorbike and set off for Mersea Island to warn the military. At the same time, a car from Mersea was heading in the opposite direction, the occupants having already seen the huge fireball themselves. It was dark and there were no street lamps in this rural location. Besides, lights usually had to remain off at night when it was known that enemy aircraft were over British skies. It is believed that neither of the vehicles were illuminated as they sped through the black country lanes. Sadly, a collision ensued and poor Mr Wright was fatally injured. His gravestone informs us that he died 'from injuries received on September 24th 1916, whilst on his way to inform the military guard of the fall of Zeppelin L33 in the parish'.

If it had not been for this tragic occurrence, the aftermath of this extraordinary incident might have resembled an episode from the TV comedy *Dad's Army*. It was not the British military that 'apprehended' the German crew, but a local bobby on his bicycle. He was the first person they confronted as they headed in the direction of Colchester in the dead of night. He must have been as surprised as any to see more than a dozen figures marching towards him. Fortunately for him, it had always been their intention to surrender. It must have also been quite a sight to see the special constable then marching the crew to nearby Peldon post office, where it was said the postmistress refused to open the premises, as she had not been issued with any special orders. At least another police constable took over from there, and the Germans were formally arrested and eventually marched to Mersea Island to be handed over to the military as prisoners of war. It is said they were temporarily housed in the church hall on the island and treated well. In fact, entertainment was laid on for them. However, by the morning, the united locals showed their solidarity by singing patriotic songs.

Much of the Zeppelin was destroyed when the Germans set it alight, though the enterprising and quick-thinking farmer whose land it crashed on is said to have charged curious sightseers the privilege of viewing the remains, the money he raised going towards the war effort. Many locals got themselves an unusual souvenir. In fact, the village church still has one hanging as a memorial – a small section of the 680ft airship itself.

Zeppelin L33 was part of a fleet that bombed London that terrible night. It was not the only one not to make it back to Germany. Another was to fall on Essex soil with even greater consequences. The entire German crew of Zeppelin L32 was buried in the churchyard at Great Burstead, near Billericay, close to where it was shot down. It appears that Little Wigborough got off lightly, even if one tragic Englishman – unbeknown to most – did lose his life in what was the most remarkable night in the history of this sleepy part of Essex.

✥ LOUGHTON ✥

The parson who made parishioners 'lopping' mad
There is nothing unusual in the fact that the parson of Loughton was asked to bless Lopping Hall at the opening ceremony towards the end of the nineteenth century.

Men of the cloth were used to carrying out this kind of service.

However, the Revd John Whitaker Maitland, who also just happened to be the lord of the manor, must have conducted the task with mixed feelings. Indirectly, he was responsible for the building of the public hall, but it came at a personal cost.

The hall was built using money paid as compensation to the parish when locals conceded their lopping rights – the freedom to cut down trees in Epping Forest for use as firewood. That was a small sacrifice to make for the residents of Loughton, however. In foregoing the right to lop, they had secured for future generations the freedom to enjoy the delights of the forest. The fact it is still a public open space for all is down to their determination in standing up against the likes of Revd Maitland of Loughton Hall. As lord of the manor, Maitland is viewed by many as the villain in what became a hard-fought battle for Epping Forest. He was one of a number of landowners who started to enclose much of the forest – illegally. They were literally extending their boundaries and selling off land to developers. It is said that Maitland fenced in more than 1,000 acres.

Epping Forest today is much reduced in size, but it may have disappeared altogether if it had not been for a group of Loughton residents, and one in particular. Thomas Willingale was a humble labourer who dared to stand up against the landowners who were stealing parts of the forest. In the mid-1860s, he broke down the fences put up by Maitland in order to carry out his ancient right to lop off the lower branches of trees for use as fuel. In doing so, Willingale – already an old man – was arrested, but eventually had his case dismissed. However, in the following year, some of his followers were found guilty of the same offence and given the choice of a fine or a spell in prison. They took the latter option as a public protest.

Queen Victoria planted a tree at High Beach to declare Epping Forest open to all, but not all were amused.

Indeed, the attention of the public had been much aroused by the actions of Willingale and his supporters. Soon some influential men and women sided with them, and the battle to save Epping Forest for the people started in earnest. Sadly, Willingale died long before Queen Victoria herself came in 1882 to officially declare the forest a public open space forever. By then the City of London Corporation had been appointed conservator. The victory had not been easy to achieve. Years of legal wrangling and debates in Parliament passed before it was finally saved. The City of London Corporation was also required to 'buy out' all the owners of land at a huge cost in order to 'nationalise' Epping Forest.

No doubt Revd Maitland was suitably compensated, but many must have questioned whether he – holy man or not – was the most suitable person to bless Lopping Hall when it opened in 1884.

❖ MAGDALEN LAVER ❖

The rector responsible for many 'conversions'
Villagers in Magdalen Laver in the nineteenth century might not have been so surprised if they saw their parson running through the school playground with an oval ball tucked under his arm.

The rector was none other than William Webb Ellis, the man who invented the sport of rugby.

One of the most important contributions Webb Ellis made to Magdalen Laver, near Harlow, during his spell here was to found the village school in 1862. No doubt he would have insisted rugby was on the curriculum!

It was during a game of football at Rugby School – the establishment from which the sport got its name – that Webb Ellis, as a student himself, famously picked up the ball and started to run with it. That was the humble beginning of rugby football.

The parish church of St Mary has a number of reminders of its famous former rector, who served for some fifteen years from 1855.

Sadly, they cannot play rugby in the playground here now, the school Webb Ellis founded having closed in 1960.

Look out for the rector of Magdalen Laver running through the churchyard with a ball tucked under his arm.

⁂ MALDON ⁂

Men are blind in their own 'cause'
Chivalrous or stupid?

One can only guess which of these best describes the most famous son of Maldon. Most are of the opinion that Byrhtnoth is the former of the two. In fact, he is portrayed as a local hero, his statue taking pride of place at Promenade Park. Indeed, there is no doubt that he was a courageous man, but some have questioned whether he was the best man to defend the town from the invading Vikings in 991.

As an Anglo-Saxon ealdorman, the people looked to Byrhtnoth when the Vikings set up camp on Northey Island, just off the Maldon coastline, in anticipation of wiping out the locals.

The outcome of the battle is no mystery. The Vikings, far stronger and in greater numbers, triumphed, as is recorded in 'The Battle of Maldon', one of the most famous poems of Old English literature, of which only a fragment survives.

What is a mystery to this day is why Byrhtnoth allowed the Vikings to cross the narrow tidal causeway to reach the mainland unmolested. The invaders would have been at their most vulnerable as they crossed the causeway in single file. It would have been easy for the locals to have picked them off one by one as they headed for the mainland.

Some have suggested that was the problem. It would have, indeed, been too easy. Byrhtnoth lived at a time when chivalry and honour were more important than life itself. Many – perhaps the more romantic – like to believe that the old Anglo-Saxon warrior was simply giving the Vikings a sporting chance. He was reluctant to slaughter men who would have had little opportunity to defend themselves. The less romantic suggest that Byrhtnoth was just plain stupid, and made a fatal tactical error in allowing the Vikings to cross and form their battle lines.

A statue in Maldon commemorates the brave, but perhaps foolhardy, Byrhtnoth.

If Byrhtnoth did display the ultimate act of chivalry, it was a code of conduct apparently very different to the one the Vikings went by. They showed little mercy on reaching the mainland. Byrhtnoth and his followers were killed, and one can only assume that the idea of the invaders retiring some of their overwhelming numbers to make the fight a little more even never once crossed their minds!

The biggest man in England

To say Edward Bright was a big man is perhaps an understatement.

He was almost 7ft – around the stomach. It meant his waist alone was wider than the height of an average man.

Needless to say, Mr Bright, who weighed in at approximately 42 stone, became more than a local curiosity. As the biggest man in England at the time, his fame spread beyond his hometown of Maldon, and prints of his portrait were sold nationally and even on the Continent.

Bright was born in 1721 and it was said he weighed at least 10 stone before the age of twelve. As a grocer, he had perhaps the perfect job, and no doubt there was not much stock left to sell! Bright not only loved fatty food, but pints of ale and wine to wash it down.

He was a genial figure and became very popular. He had a good word for all who passed by as he sat outside his shop in the high street. Sadly, that was about all he could do in the end. Walking became a big problem and he was not even able to mount a horse in his latter days – fortunately for the horse!

The former Maldon home of a larger-than-life character.

Standing at only 5ft 9in, Bright is said to have measured about 2ft 8in around the middle of his legs and 2ft 2in around the middle of his arms. Famously, one of his fellow traders bet another that five grown men could button themselves inside Bright's enormous waistcoat without bursting a stitch. He won his bet – as seven succeeded in doing so.

Seven men could fit within the waistcoat of Edward Bright, as this memorial highlights.

Not surprisingly, Bright's weight brought many health problems, and he died before he was thirty. There was much talk upon his death as to how he would be laid to rest. A special oversize coffin had to be made, but the biggest problem was getting the corpse from the bedroom to the church. The staircase was too narrow and besides, no six men would have the combined strength to be able to bear the coffin. In the end, a way had to be cut through the wall and staircase before it could be lowered to the ground floor. The shop door also had to be widened. Lowering the coffin into the vault at the church also proved tricky, a triangle and pulley eventually doing the job.

A man of many words

We know benefactor Thomas Plume had a wide range of interests, thanks to the 8,000 or so books he left to the town of Maldon.

They are books on all kinds of subjects. However, for the fact that his personal library was so extensive, we can perhaps safely assume that his first love was books themselves.

The amazing collection of mostly sixteenth- and seventeenth-century works is housed in a building Plume himself constructed from the ruins of St Peter's Church. His personal library is still open to the public, as Plume intended it to be when he died in 1704.

Plume was born at Maldon in 1630, but went on to serve people elsewhere in his posts as a clergyman and later archdeacon. However, the residents of Maldon certainly benefited too. Not only did he bequeath his valuable library to the town, but he also left lots of money for worthy projects. However, it is his books – which now form one of the most important libraries in England – that attract most attention. Theological works are unsurprisingly prominent, though there are also books on travel, mathematics, history, medicine and astronomy.

Like Billio

Whatever people may have thought of Puritan preacher Joseph Billio, you could not have said he was dull.

It is unlikely many fell asleep listening to his sermons. The manner in which he delivered his message of fire and brimstone made him the talk of the town of Maldon. Such was his zeal and passion when addressing his congregation, his reputation spread and he became responsible for a phrase in the English language that is still in use today. To do something 'like billio' means to exert oneself in an extreme way. You will still hear people say they ran like billio, for example.

Joseph Billio was a man full of fervour and energy, a skilled orator. It is said he had no problem filling the Nonconformist meeting house that he founded in Maldon in 1696. It seems no one could preach quite like Billio!

Maldon United Reformed Church now occupies the Market Hill site where Billio once took to the pulpit.

⁓ MERSEA ISLAND ⁓

Oh! I don't like to be beside the seaside
Tourism chiefs do not have to work too hard to encourage visitors to the beaches of Mersea Island these days.

However, they certainly would have had to work a bit harder in the late nineteenth century.

Fortunately, things have changed a lot since famous author Sabine Baring-Gould was rector here for some ten years from the early 1870s. His autobiographical *Further Reminiscences* contains a chapter titled 'Ten Years on the Mud', which does not paint the greatest picture of the island. The clergyman was so disparaging towards his home and the neighbours he was supposed to be serving that it is a mystery why he stayed for as long as he did. He described Mersea Island as 'bleak and inhospitable – the ends of the earth'. He added: 'I cannot say that I either liked the place or became attached to the people.' He even went as far as to suggest that his parishioners were 'dull', 'stupid' and 'suspicious', while the children were 'uncouth'. The Essex accent is not to everyone's taste and Baring-Gould found the dialect to be 'markedly vulgar'.

Some might suggest the rector of East Mersea was a bit of a snob. He was certainly an educated man, a scholar, and those he had to share the island with

Beach huts on Mersea Island suggest tourists like the place more than a famous former rector did.

were not. He bemoaned the fact that there was no resident gentry. 'As far as I could see there were not many persons of value as readers and thinkers, with whom to make friends,' he wrote.

He even found the vicar of neighbouring West Mersea to be dull.

The smell of the place did not help matters. Mersea Island was used as a dumping ground for the 'sweepings of London streets' – the muck from the many horses in the capital being shipped here and used as manure for the surrounding fields. 'The stench was horrible,' Baring-Gould complained. The muck also attracted swarms of mosquitoes, which could not have been good for health. The man of God went as far as to suggest that disease might have been an explanation as to why the residents were not the sharpest crayons in the box. He wrote: 'My impression was that generations afflicted with these complaints [ague and rheumatism] acquired in the marshes had lowered the physique and mental development of the islanders.'

Baring-Gould later used the island as the setting for his bleak novel *Mehalah*, which was published in 1880. He is best remembered for his many hymns. 'Onward, Christian Soldiers', he claimed, was written in less than 15 minutes. That might explain why he was such a prolific writer. It is said that during his lifetime, more of his books were in the British Library than those of any other author.

It is perhaps something of a mystery why Sabine Baring-Gould is so fondly remembered on Mersea Island, as it appears from his memoirs that – unlike many tourists today – he could not wait to get off it!

𝓃

⚜ NAVESTOCK ⚜

The reluctant prime minister
Few are aware that a former prime minister lies at rest in the parish church at Navestock.

You perhaps cannot blame people for being oblivious to the fact – or for not even having heard of the man himself – as James Waldegrave, 2nd Earl Waldegrave, only held the top government position for some five days.

James Waldegrave was probably relieved that his term of office was so brief. He did not want the job in the first place. He only allowed himself to be nominated to please the king, who was not only the monarch, but also a personal friend. He was propelled into the spotlight following the resignation of the Duke of Newcastle in 1756. Waldegrave – a member of a prominent Essex family who held the manor of Navestock, near Brentwood – attempted to form a government between the 8th and 12th of June the following year. The statesman was not successful and stepped down. It is said he feared his friendship with the king would suffer if he were in charge of the government, as had been the case with many who had come before him.

So short was Waldegrave's reign that he sometimes does not even appear on the list of former British prime ministers, some claiming he did not officially take up office.

Incredibly, there was another who enjoyed an even shorter reign. William Pulteney, 1st Earl of Bath, lasted just two days!

⚜ NEWPORT ⚜

The king has been to Nell and back
There would have been plenty of room for the entourage of Charles II when he came to grand Audley End, near Saffron Walden.

It was one of the biggest houses in England.

However, at least one person closer than most to the king had to lodge at nearby Newport, according to tradition. It would not have been the done thing if Charles had brought his long-time mistress to Audley End, which

Did 'pretty, witty Nell' secretly lodge here while the king resided at nearby Audley End?

meant Nell Gwyn was dropped off at a tavern in that particular village. No doubt the monarch, at a convenient moment, made his excuses and went off in search of Nell.

The Crown House still stands. The building, formerly the Crown inn, is much older than 1692; this date, clearly visible above the door, presumably refers to a makeover it received in that year. There is no evidence to confirm that 'pretty, witty Nell' ever lodged here, but it is easy to imagine the king sneaking away from Audley End to join Nell for a quick half and anything else they might fancy!

❖ ONGAR ❖

Chipping Ongar, I presume?

Explorer David Livingstone might have trekked across Africa and found the Victoria Falls, but few know that he got lost in Essex and struggled to find his way home.

Livingstone was sent to Chipping Ongar in 1838 as part of his training to become a missionary. He resided at what is now Livingstone Cottages in the high street for more than a year under the tutorship of the Revd Richard Cecil, who was minister of the Congregational Church here.

Livingstone was already a keen walker and possessed the sense of adventure he would need in later life when he crossed Africa, from the Atlantic Ocean to the Indian Ocean, walking thousands of miles in the process.

While in Chipping Ongar, Livingstone decided to walk to London to visit a sick relative – a round trip of some 50 miles. Things did not start that well. He set off in the early hours of the morning and, in the darkness, managed to stumble down a deep ditch. Undeterred, no doubt already displaying the resilience that would be invaluable to him in Africa, Livingstone battled on. He could not have had long in the capital before it was time to make the return journey. However, the darkness and fog soon descended again, and Livingstone discovered that he was well and truly lost. He decided to give up and look for a ditch where he could lie down for the night. One can only assume he could not find one, not even the one he had fallen into on the outward journey! What he did find, much to his relief, was a direction post at Stanford Rivers that pointed the way to Chipping Ongar. After getting his bearings, Livingstone arrived home in the middle of the night, footsore and weary; he was the butt of many jokes from his fellow students the next morning, though they were also amazed by his energy and determination.

Livingstone lost something else in Essex too – his words. And it nearly cost him his dream of moving abroad as a missionary.

As part of his training, when the normal minister at Stanford Rivers fell ill, Livingstone was asked to deputise. Fortunately, he had no problem finding the

The Chipping Ongar home of explorer David Livingstone that he had trouble finding on one occasion.

Independent Chapel and was very excited at the prospect of preaching his first sermon. He was obviously a little nervous too. After reading the Bible verse, the young Livingstone found he had forgotten everything he was intending to say. Filled with terror, he apologised to the stunned congregation and fled the building.

Fortunately, Livingstone was given a second chance, and no doubt his experiences at Chipping Ongar became invaluable to him in later life. Indeed, those who may think Ongar is a far cry from Africa should take note of some words from the great man himself. He certainly never forgot his old Essex haunt. In a letter, he wrote: 'At Algoa Bay … the village is as like Ongar in Essex as regards population and appearance as two places can be.'

No doubt he renamed it in his heart too … Chipping Algoa, I presume?

Arranging deck 'prayers' on the Titanic

Few people in Chipping Ongar are aware that a former resident of the town went down with the ill-fated *Titanic*. That fact alone would perhaps not be enough to ensure that people living more than 100 years after the tragedy should know.

However, it is perhaps something of a mystery why the heroic story of Father Thomas Byles – who was declared a martyr of the Roman Catholic Church – is not shouted from the rooftops here. Less worthy individuals have been immortalised in stone or bronze, but there is no statue of Father Byles, and most residents shake their heads when asked if they have even heard of him.

However, worshippers at St Helen's Roman Catholic Church, hidden just off the high street, will know all about Father Byles. He was priest here when he boarded the *Titanic* to travel to New York to officiate at his brother's wedding.

According to eyewitnesses, Father Byles was praying when the ship hit an iceberg. When he realised how serious the situation was, he went to the aid of the third-class passengers. Amid the chaos and panic, the priest tried to bring calm, giving absolutions and blessings to those who wanted them. He is said to have helped people into the lifeboats and refused the pleas of others to get in one himself. Once the last lifeboat had left the stricken ship, Father Byles, along with some 100 people, was left stranded at the stern of the vessel. With frightened passengers kneeling around him, Father Byles led prayers and gave a general absolution. One eyewitness who escaped on one of the lifeboats reported hearing, in the distance, the brave and faithful priest leading the singing of a hymn as the *Titanic* slipped into the icy ocean. The hymn was 'Nearer, My God, to Thee', the work of Harlow-born scribe Sarah Flower Adams.

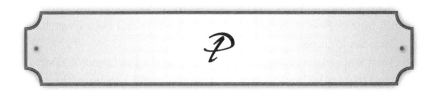

⁂ PAGLESHAM ⁂

God helps those who help themselves
There may be a reason why there are no records of the transgressions of Paglesham smuggler William 'Hard Apple' Blyth.

It is said that this king of the Essex smugglers just happened to be a churchwarden and a member of the parish council. He was also a grocer and there is a romantic notion of him using pages torn from the parish register to wrap up his smuggled bacon.

There are many perhaps farcical tales about the life of Blyth that have stood the test of time. He is also supposed to have fought a bull with his bare hands and, once he had finished his drink at the local Punch Bowl inn, he is said to have consumed his glass as well! All in all, it appears he was a tough man and it is hardly surprising that he should gain legendary status in this part of the world.

The little we know about Blyth – who was never actually charged for smuggling – is from the memoirs of local magistrate John Harriott, which were published in the early part of the nineteenth century. In the work, Harriott recounts occasions when Blyth escaped from the clutches of the customs officers. One can assume Blyth got his nickname from his ability to consume vast amounts of liquor. That may have been to his advantage on one occasion. After being apprehended by revenue men, Blyth is said to have persuaded the officers – more than a few were probably open to a bribe – to have a drink with him and to discuss just how many of his smuggled tubs of spirit should be seized. At the end of the session, it is said the officers were so drunk that Blyth was able to put all the tubs they had seized back onto his boat, and even managed to gain a few extra that had been lying on the revenue cutter from another operation.

Blyth is depicted on the village sign at Paglesham, a remote spot, east of Rochford, that can probably claim to have been the home of smuggling in Essex. It is said the entire village was involved in the 'free trade' in some way. Even the parish church was allegedly used to store smuggled goods, though in Blyth's role as churchwarden, that is perhaps not too much of a surprise.

The theory of dissolution

Somewhere just off the Essex coast is thought to lie one of the most famous ships in British history. Few are aware of its existence here and even fewer have any idea of its exact location.

The rural and isolated village of Paglesham was the last home of HMS *Beagle* – the vessel that took Charles Darwin round the world. On-board, he collected the evidence that would shape his revolutionary theories of evolution that so changed Victorian thinking.

The *Beagle* is believed to now sit under several metres of estuary mud somewhere close to, or on, Potton Island. It is perhaps a sad end to such an illustrious career. Following Darwin's voyage, the *Beagle* was employed in various occupations, before becoming a watch vessel for Customs & Excise. It was moored at Paglesham and given the less glamorous name *Southend Watch Vessel No. 7*.

The area was once a hotbed for smuggling and there is little doubt that *No. 7* would have been kept very busy. It is believed the ship spent its final days ashore on a fixed mooring when it served as the home of customs officers and their families. It is thought the vessel was sold for scrap, but not scrapped, its remains located at the beginning of this century. There have indeed been suggestions of attempting to retrieve what might be left of the ship. Who knows, remote Paglesham might one day have its own *Mary Rose* to attract visitors from all over the world.

Does the *Beagle* lie in mud with other decaying vessels at Paglesham?

⚜ PURFLEET ⚜

The queen who had the wrong shoes on

There is a charming – but fanciful – legend that Purfleet was so named by none other than Queen Elizabeth.

She famously rallied the troops at Tilbury in 1588 in anticipation of an attack from the Spanish Armada. On her way from London, it is said her royal barge was caught in a terrible storm as it made its way along the Thames. She was forced to vacate the vessel and seek shelter on land. Concerned for the welfare of her ships at Tilbury, the monarch is said to have climbed up a hill and cast her gaze in the direction of her fleet. The sight that greeted her must not have been good. No doubt her ships were being buffeted by large waves and a gale-force wind, prompting her to shriek: 'Oh, my poor fleet!'

There is another version – even more delightful – but more than likely the work of a local wag. It is said that on climbing the hill, the queen was more concerned about her own welfare than that of her fleet. No doubt she had not been wearing the most appropriate shoes for such a trek and is said to have wailed: 'Oh, my poor feet!'

Believe what version you wish – if any.

⚜ PURLEIGH ⚜

'Pint' the way to the White House

You might be surprised to hear an American accent in the archetypal English village of Purleigh. However, a number of visitors from across the Atlantic come here to trace the roots of one of America's greatest sons.

It is not widely known beyond Purleigh that the village was once home to the great-great-grandfather of George Washington – first president of the United States.

Lawrence Washington was rector here for some ten years from the early 1630s. In fact, the tower of the parish church was repaired at the expense of US residents in honour of one of their ancestors.

The Revd Washington served the village of Purleigh, near Maldon, at a difficult time. He had Royalist sympathies and might have stayed longer if the Parliamentarians had not ejected him from his living. Those God-fearing Puritans, who opposed what many believed were simple and harmless pleasures, were particularly against alcohol, believing it to be the brew of the Devil. They accused Revd Washington of being 'a common frequenter of ale-houses'. If that was not bad enough, they went further to condemn him for 'not only himself sitting daily tippling there but also encouraging others in the same beastly vice'.

The ardent Protestants, it has to be said, often looked for any excuse to eject a loyalist clergyman during those troubled times and it is more than possible that they painted a blacker portrait of the rector than was just. By other accounts, Revd Washington was deemed to be a pious and worthy man.

The Washingtons fell into poverty and Lawrence eventually died in the early 1650s. Two of his sons moved to America a few years after the death of their father. John – one of them – settled in Virginia. He married and his great-grandson was none other than George Washington himself.

A portrait of George Washington hangs in the church at Purleigh.

Lawrence Washington was buried at the Church of All Saints in Maldon, where there is a commemorative window, a gift from the United States.

The Russian revelation

You might hear an American accent in Purleigh today, but in days gone by you were more likely to come across a Russian one.

And, at the end of the nineteenth century, you might have even crossed paths with a certain Leo Tolstoy, author of *War and Peace*.

Not many know that a little part of Russia once existed here. Tolstoy came to Purleigh to visit a community set up to follow his ideals and principles. The Purleigh Colony existed for a few years from 1896, stemming from the Croydon Brotherhood Church that had become the leading centre for Tolstoyism in Britain. Those who made their home at Purleigh attempted to be self-sufficient. It meant they carried out all agricultural work themselves. It was effectively a Christian anarchist group, rejecting all types of violence, but also all forms of government and authority. Tolstoy himself rejected the state and its institutions, including the Church, police and army. Some of the members at Purleigh had actually lived in Russia and were personally acquainted with Tolstoy. A number had fled their homeland due to political persecution. Tolstoy came to visit the colony in 1898.

⁕ QUENDON ⁕

'Poor Robin' saved Christmas

Few know that if it had not been for an obscure seventeenth-century writer from the rural village of Quendon, we might not 'celebrate' Christmas every year. It would have probably been very different at any rate.

If William Winstanley is not remembered for his literary output, he should at least be hailed as the man who saved Christmas.

While most think it was the Grinch that stole Christmas, it was, in fact, Oliver Cromwell. During the Commonwealth, the pious Puritan leader supported a ban imposed by Parliament, believing that the true meaning of Christmas had become lost within all the packaging. People were now using the religious day as an excuse to party. It had become a time to eat and drink to excess. Even the word 'Christmas' was offensive to the Puritans, 'Christ's mass' being too closely associated with Roman Catholicism. It was changed to 'Christ tide' and, instead of days of feasting, people were encouraged to partake in a day of fasting! Those who did not obey could have found themselves in trouble.

The Winstanleys of Quendon, south of Saffron Walden, were Royalists. They liked Christmas, as they knew it, so much so that they were willing to take the risk of upsetting Cromwell and his government.

From their 'Berries' home, they continued to celebrate Christmas in secret, with fellow supporters of the old festivities joining them for carols and games, not to mention plenty of food and drink. They had to celebrate in secret for many years. For the entire time the country was a Republic, Christmas (as we know it now) remained officially banned in Britain.

It seems the people soon got used to 'Christ tide'. Even when Charles II was restored to the throne, the public were reluctant to go back to their old ways. Winstanley started a personal campaign to see Christmas restored. The writer was sometimes known as the 'Barber Poet', having given up the razor for a pen, though he became more widely known as 'Poor Robin' – the pseudonym he used when penning his many almanacs and chapbooks, a field in which he became something of a pioneer. He used this medium to laud the joys of

Christmas in the hope people would recover their enthusiasm for it. Winstanley even told people how they should celebrate Christmas. Through his writing, he suggested what should be eaten at the dinner table – turkey, geese and mince pies among the fare we are so familiar with today. He also advocated playing games; plenty of carol singing; and even ghost stories around a log fire. Winstanley was still promoting the joys of Christmas at the time of his death in 1698, though by then the festival was already starting to return to how it was before the Puritans came to power.

So, when you are feasting on turkey and singing carols around the log fire this December, do not forget to raise a glass to William Winstanley – now lying at rest in Quendon – the man who saved Christmas.

However, so commercialised has Christmas become, some might feel Oliver 'Ebenezer Scrooge' Cromwell had hit the nail on the head, and was simply doing us all a favour. Bah, Humbug!

✥ RAYNE ✥

You'll cross that 'Bridge' when you come to Harvard

There are some who say the oldest and most famous university in the United States should be named after an Essex man.

It was John Bridge – and not John Harvard – who founded the school that became the seat of learning famous all over the world.

The Bridge family home was a property called Turners in Stone Street, Rayne, near Braintree. John Bridge set sail for America on-board the *Lyon* in 1631. He was a Puritan and one of a group of religious dissenters seeking a new home where they could worship in the way they saw fit. The Braintree Company, as

The former home of the man who founded Harvard University.

they became known, ensured the Essex town now lives on in the US too, with a place there sharing the name. Another to sail on the *Lyon* was an ancestor of John Adams, second president of the United States. Adams' son – John Quincy Adams – later became the country's sixth president.

Bridge eventually settled in New Town where he became a leading citizen. Among his many achievements was the establishment of a school that developed into Harvard University. He supervised what was then the first public school established in the new colony.

The name 'Harvard' came from a former Cambridge graduate. John Harvard was the first benefactor of that great seat of learning. Following his death in 1638 he left his library and half his estate to the institution. That was enough to ensure the then college was named after him. New Town was also changed to Cambridge in honour of John Harvard. Bridge is not forgotten for his efforts in founding Harvard – there is a fine statue in his honour – though it is perhaps a little unjust that most of the glory should go the way of another.

⚜ RIVENHALL ⚜

A 'how to' book on farming … by a very unsuccessful farmer
Sixteenth-century poet and farmer Thomas Tusser showed others how to succeed, but was unable to do so himself. This apparently lousy farmer led fellow agricultural workers to prosperity, but died penniless in prison.

Readers could not get enough of his tips on farming and gardening, his instructions and proverbs collected in *Five Hundred Points of Good Husbandry*. The long rhyming poem was a big hit and ran to several editions, first starting life as just 100 points.

Tusser was born at Rivenhall, near Witham, though mostly farmed just over the border in Suffolk. He is believed to have been responsible for introducing the cultivation of barley, but presumably not to any commercial success. It appears the wisdom he imparted to his readers was inspired by his own bad experiences. None of his own business ventures seemed to work out for him and he died in a London prison for debt in 1580.

Historian Thomas Fuller wrote that Tusser 'spread his bread with all sorts of butter, yet none would stick thereon'.

Tusser might have failed in his life on the land, but his celebrated work is still much quoted. It was enlarged during his own lifetime to include points of housewifery too. Sadly, Tusser appears to have made little money from his writing, and certainly even less through his failed farming ventures. His charming work is unique in English literature, providing an incomparable portrait of sixteenth-century agricultural life. It was one of the first 'how to' books ever written. It is just a shame Tusser could not put his own good advice into practice, though farmers and gardeners today owe a great debt to him. What a shame he could not have claimed it in his own lifetime and thus been spared those final tragic days in a debtors' prison.

⚜ ROYDON ⚜

More's the pity

Sir Thomas More – that now famous saint of the Roman Catholic Church – came to the village of Roydon, near Harlow, for the love of not one woman, but two.

The once grand Nether Hall was home to two sisters who caught the eye of the influential More. It is said he first fell for the second daughter of the Colt family, but ended up marrying her elder sister.

In those days, families liked to see their daughters married off one by one, starting with the eldest. The story goes that More, while courting the second daughter, started to believe that marriage with her would result in her elder sister feeling much shame, having been left on the shelf. Full of pity for the elder sibling, he is said to have turned his attention to her. And so, in 1505, More married Jane Colt and not her younger sister, the one who had caught his eye in the first place. An admirable deed it may have been on More's part, but you cannot help but sympathise with the woman who now found herself discarded. It is said Jane was almost ten years the junior of More. That gap would have been even greater if he had married his first love, though husbands were often old enough to be their wife's father – or even grandfather – in those days.

Sadly, More had to marry again anyway, as Jane died in 1511.

⚜ RUNWELL ⚜

The wages of sin is death

There is an old tradition that the Devil is not allowed to enter through the south door of a church. The north side has always been considered the haunt of Old Nick. Criminals, the unbaptised and the excommunicated were usually buried on that side of the churchyard for this reason.

In the parish church at Runwell, near Wickford, it appears the Devil flouted the rules a little. Many years ago he made a grab for a corrupt priest called Rainaldus. It is said the man of the cloth was in the habit of practising black magic. For this sin, the Devil believed his soul now belonged to him and he wasted little time in trying to obtain it. While Rainaldus was leading his congregation in what was probably another alternative service, the Devil appeared and lunged for the priest.

Rainaldus met his fate in the church porch at Runwell.

The terrified parishioners headed for the sanctuary of the south door, Rainaldus hot on their heels. It is said they got there just in time, closing the door behind them. Old Nick was furious and gave the door a mighty thump, leaving on it a huge imprint of his claws. That was at least the explanation given to subsequent parishioners about a strange mark on the door.

Alas for poor Rainaldus, the Devil was not to be outdone. Knowing he would not be able to go through the door, he is said to have squeezed through the squint, a tiny hole in the wall of the church from which lepers were allowed to watch the service. The frightened congregation had long fled, but it is said the Devil, once on the outside of the building, shut the outer door so that Rainaldus was trapped in the porch. When the parishioners returned, there was no sign of their priest, just a vile puddle of steaming liquid. In it was a small flint stone, in the shape of a head, which bore the inscription 'the wages of sin is death'.

That is not quite the end of the story. In 1944, a stone was discovered in the churchyard, shaped as the legend describes.

❧ SAFFRON WALDEN ☙

The practical joker who became a hero to mariners

It is both ironic and tragic that the greatest achievement of Henry Winstanley was to cost him his life.

Not many know that until the celebrated engineer took it upon himself to construct the first lighthouse at the infamous Eddystone Rocks, Winstanley had a reputation for being an eccentric practical joker. Few took him seriously and his home in Littlebury, on the outskirts of Saffron Walden, became a house of fun. It was filled with the most bizarre inventions and tricks. There were intricate mechanical devices and clockwork gadgets, even trapdoors and a chair that would grip the unwary occupant with its arms as they sat down. People came from miles to view his strange and whimsical creations. In fact, Winstanley eventually opened his doors to the paying public to help fund his ambitious project for a lighthouse.

Most were of the opinion that not even the greatest engineer would be able to build a beacon at treacherous Eddystone Rocks, some 14 miles off the coast of Plymouth. Many great minds turned down the challenge. No doubt, there were more than one or two sniggers when the quirky and outlandish Winstanley, known for his practical jokes, announced he was to take on the 'impossible' task. The lighthouse took some three years to build and at one point work was interrupted when a French privateer captured Winstanley and took him prisoner. However, as soon as the king of France discovered that Winstanley was trying to build a lighthouse in an area that had claimed the lives of so many, the noble engineer was released and allowed to continue with his work.

After overcoming trying conditions and numerous setbacks, the wooden lighthouse was operational by 1698. Countless lives were undoubtedly saved in the years it stood. Winstanley was of the belief that it would survive the fiercest of storms, and he even longed for one, in order to prove to the world that it would withstand anything nature could throw at it. Sadly, his wish came true, in the form of probably the greatest tempest that has ever hit Britain. Despite the warnings, Winstanley chose to stay in the lighthouse during that fateful night in 1703.

By the following morning, the first Eddystone lighthouse had been swept out to sea, taking its creator with it.

That it stood for so long was a remarkable achievement, however. No ships were lost during its reign and its importance was highlighted just a few days after its demise, when a vessel ran aground with the loss of most of its crew.

Encouraged by the success of Winstanley, another lighthouse was built and there is still one on Eddystone Rocks to this day. It is a fitting tribute to a remarkable man who went from being a figure of fun to a national hero.

It will all end in tears ... of laughter

Those who dare to predict the end of the world put themselves in a no-win situation. Get it wrong and they are open to ridicule. Get it right and there is every chance they will not have much opportunity to bask in their triumph.

Needless to say, Richard Harvey, son of a Saffron Walden ropemaker, got it wrong. He was so mocked when his prophecy did not come true, it is a wonder he never borrowed some of his father's rope and made a noose for himself.

Richard, brother of the more famous scholar Gabriel, certainly put himself in the line of fire with his prediction, which he put on paper at the end of 1582 while at the Saffron Walden home of his father. Richard had a keen interest in astrology. He was only in his early twenties when he saw something catastrophic in the stars. He wasted no time in warning people and hastily penned *An astrological discourse upon the great and notable conjunction of the two superior planets, Saturn and Jupiter, which shall happen the 28th day of April, 1583, with a brief declaration of the effects, which the late eclipse of the sun 1582 is yet hereafter to work.*

You would have thought that someone predicting something as dramatic and awful as the beginning of the end of the world could have come up with a snappier title. Nevertheless, the work caught the attention of the public. In fact, it caused much consternation throughout the country. So popular did the work become, and so seriously was it taken, that people were said to be literally on their knees in prayer as the clock struck 12 noon on the fateful day, the time Harvey predicted gales and floods would start to cause havoc on earth.

Perhaps foolishly, he had confidently added in his work: 'If these things fall not out in every point as I have written, let me forever hereafter lose the credit of my astronomy.'

Needless to say ... he did.

An a 'maze'ing mystery

It should not take the average person too long to find their way out of the famous turf maze at Saffron Walden. However, it will take them a lot longer to come up with the reason why it is here.

Many have put forward theories as to its origin, but there is no way of obtaining the definitive answer. It remains a local mystery that is unlikely to be solved.

What we do know is that the maze is the largest public turf maze in England and also one of the oldest. The earliest record of its existence dates back to the end of the seventeenth century, but some think it could be some 800 years old. The very nature of turf mazes means it is difficult to glean much information from them. Grass grows and they have to be re-cut. Town records reveal that the Saffron Walden maze was re-cut at a cost of 15*s* in 1699. That is the earliest record of it.

In a turf maze, the grass becomes the 'walls', which means that those attempting to find the centre or their way out can see all of the winding paths before them, unlike in a hedge maze. The most obvious disadvantage – or advantage – is that you can cheat and 'get out' by just walking away.

Historians know maze patterns go back as far as Celtic times. They were drawn on doors and at entrances in an attempt to ward off evil spirits, the idea being that the demon would be confused by the pattern. Mazes may have been a development of this idea. It is believed that monks in the Middle Ages walked them as a form of penance. Some have suggested that the Saffron Walden turf maze, situated not too far from the parish church, may have originally had some religious purpose. One theory is that the maze symbolised a Christian's walk in life. Heaven is only found if the individual remains on the correct path. Deviate from it – through sin – and they will come to a dead end. The only way is God's way.

Children and adults still enjoy Saffron Walden's mysterious turf maze.

One non-religious theory is that the maze was used for maidens to test the love of their suitors. She would stand in the centre and her lover had to reach her. Those who refused to give up proved their love for her. The maze might have even been used to settle an argument. Two rivals after the same woman might have raced each other, the man who got there first able to claim his 'prize'.

Certainly, by Victorian times, the main function of the maze was pleasure. Children – and adults – still get much fun from Saffron Walden's unusual attraction. And, once you have conquered this maze, you can always try another. The town is probably unique for having not one but two mazes. The hedge maze in Bridge End Gardens is a little younger and less mysterious, however, having only been created during the Victorian age.

❧ SANDON ❧

The Gretna Green of Essex

Eloping couples, or those in need of a shotgun wedding during the first half of the seventeenth century, did not need to travel all the way to Gretna Green.

Those in the south only needed to head for a small village on the outskirts of Chelmsford.

Sandon was the parish of Revd Gilbert Dillingham. He gained quite a reputation for his willingness to marry couples – no questions asked. Hundreds of runaway brides turned up on his doorstep, the word having spread that the rector of St Andrew's Church was happy to do the honours, for the right fee, of course.

❧ SHOEBURYNESS ❧

The Hitchhiker's Guide to the Celestial City

Arthur Dent, a former rector of South Shoebury, is little remembered today. Nor is his most famous book. However, without that book, one of the greatest works of literature would probably not have been written.

Dent's *The Plain Man's Path-way to Heaven* was to set up a memorable chain of events in the life of none other than John Bunyan, author of the greatest religious allegory of all time – *The Pilgrim's Progress*.

Dent's religious book was itself a bestseller and ran to many editions following his death in 1607. One person who owned a copy was the future Mrs Bunyan. It is said that on her marriage to the Puritan scribe, she brought with her just two possessions – both books – one of which was *The Plain Man's Path-way to Heaven*.

Husband John, on reading the books (the other was Lewis Bayly's *The Practice of Piety*), became convinced he was a sinner and destined for eternal damnation.

Puritans like Dent were of the belief that many seemingly harmless pastimes were sinful. Bunyan famously gave up his favourite activities of dancing and bell-ringing, and devoted himself to studying the Bible. It ultimately led to his spiritual conversion, which led to a spell behind prison for his Nonconformism, which then led to the penning of *The Pilgrim's Progress*.

So while the Revd Arthur Dent may be looked upon as a bit of a spoilsport who encouraged people to stop having fun, one should perhaps acknowledge that without him one of the finest and most inspiring books would probably never have come to light. However, his name is now more commonly associated with the chief character of *The Hitchhiker's Guide to the Galaxy*. Douglas Adams, author of that classic science-fiction adventure, is said to have named Arthur Dent after this now almost-forgotten man of the cloth.

❧ SILVER END ❧

The man who built a village
One day in the 1920s, a man was driving between his two factories in Braintree and Witham when he turned off the main road. He reached an isolated hamlet of just a few cottages, surrounded by acres of fields.

More than a few people raised their eyebrows in surprise when that man bought all the land and announced that he was to create a garden village there. Certainly, if that man had not been the successful industrialist and philanthropist Francis Crittall, many would have thought him mad. But Crittall had already come a long way from his early days as a Braintree ironmonger. Concerned at seeing his mother hurt herself as she struggled to open a heavy wooden window, he started the manufacture of metal window frames. Crittall soon became a household name. So successful did his business become, it is said that more than half of the population of Braintree, amounting to thousands of people, was made up of his employees and their families. The town was bursting at the seams. And so Crittall – known among his workforce as 'The Guv'nor' – came up with the wacky idea of moving his employees to a self-sufficient and purpose-built village in the country.

Crittall had always dreamed of creating a place where his expanding workforce could live. After buying the land, he wrote to his employees informing them of the proposed development. That there was such a positive and overwhelming response to the plan highlights the regard with which Crittall was held among his workforce.

Hundreds of homes were built. Crittall built one there for himself too. A village hall was opened to cater for the needs of the new residents, though it was a village hall like no other. Within it were a 400-seat theatre and cinema, dance

The Silver End home of the remarkable Francis Crittall.

floor, restaurant, health clinic, lecture room, library, billiard room and much more. It was more like a holiday camp and became the largest village hall in the country. Villagers had no need to go elsewhere for anything. Food was farmed locally. There was a slaughterhouse and a sausage factory. The community even had its own newspaper.

By the early 1930s, the garden village of Silver End was completed. Today, many of the surviving buildings are of national importance due to the modernist architecture, a style much criticised at the time but copied throughout the country.

A small parts factory was also established at Silver End – set up to provide light work for those left disabled following the First World War. Crittall was an unusual employer at the time – he really cared for his workers. They were paid much more than the average wage and received perks other employees throughout Britain could only dream of. For Crittall, the welfare of his people was of paramount importance. It is said he was the first man in England to introduce a five-day working week. He believed his employees would work harder having benefited from two days off.

There are many eccentric dreamers in the world, but Crittall was a man who made sure his dreams came true. There can have been few people who could say they were responsible for building an entire village.

⚜ SOUTHEND-ON-SEA ⚜

The world is not your oyster

It is not widely known that the Essex coastline was plundered by the Armada.

However, this was not the Spanish one that prompted Queen Elizabeth to rally her troops just along the coast at Tilbury, delivering her most famous speech in anticipation of an attack that did not materialise. This was the Kent Armada!

In 1724, a fleet made up of some 500 fishermen from Kent descended on the foreshore at what is now Southend-on-Sea. Essex has always been famous for its oysters and this is what its Kent neighbours had come for. The Essex oyster beds were looked upon with envy. Almost all of the coastline from Shoeburyness to Leigh-on-Sea was devoted to the cultivation of oysters. The Kent men, led by the mayor of Queenborough, claimed the oyster beds were public property. They came with flags flying and guns firing. The Riot Act was read on the foreshore to the invaders. There was not thought to be any violence, but the Essex men could not prevent the Kent raiders from filling their boats with oysters over the next few days. It is said many tons were plundered and much damage was caused in the process.

The matter was eventually settled in court in favour of the Essex men. The law judged that their Kent neighbours had no right to the Essex oysters, and the audacious raiders were forced to pay damages.

Hell's bells!

It is not a good idea to live close to the parish church if you do not like the sound of bells. However, that could be a problem if you are the vicar.

The Revd Frederick Nolan came to serve the parish of Prittlewell, now part of Southend-on-Sea, in the first part of the nineteenth century. On his arrival in 1822, it is said he was warned that the bells of St Mary's Church were in regular use, its bell-ringers having a fine reputation. Of course, being the vicar, Revd Nolan lived closer than anybody to the bell tower. At first he obligingly agreed to the campanologists' requests, such as permission to start ringing the bells from 5 a.m. However, when he asked them if they could wait until after 8 a.m. to start ringing, his polite request was refused. Relations between both parties subsequently deteriorated over the years.

The Revd Nolan was a scholar and very different to most of his uneducated parishioners. He spent much of his time writing and published many obscure works of literature, even setting up a printing press in the vicarage. The seemingly endless ringing of bells at all hours proved detrimental to his labours, though it appears he endured them for some eighteen years. However, one day in 1840, he finally snapped. After the bells had been ringing for some considerable time, the frustrated vicar seized a knife and rushed up the belfry stairs. Much to the amazement of the bell-ringers, he started slashing at the bell ropes and had to be restrained.

The authorities became involved in the dispute and told both parties to keep the peace. The Revd Nolan soon went to the extent of locking the church door and placing a constable on guard outside. The bell-ringers, now denied access to the bells, were livid and smashed the vicarage windows, while Revd Nolan armed himself with a pistol and fired warning shots to get them to disperse. Not to be outdone, the bell-ringers finally managed to reach the belfry via another route, by scaling the church roof. It was too much for the vicar, who this time aimed his gun at the culprits themselves.

Some of the bell-ringers, who by law were supposed to get permission from the vicar to ring the church bells, were summoned to appear before a Church court, but never turned up. They were fined for contempt, while the ringleader (no pun intended) was arrested and jailed for a few months for not paying the fine. He was only released on condition that neither he nor his allies would hassle the vicar again.

Things seemingly calmed down, as Revd Nolan remained vicar for many more years, but it is fair to say he was probably not the most popular person following the incident, and you wonder how many of his parishioners turned up for church on Sunday mornings!

⚜ SOUTHMINSTER ⚜

The Victory 'sign'

Most wedding parties signing the marriage register at Southminster Church probably took little interest in the piece of furniture reputedly used for the purpose. Some might have even thought it looked a little worse for wear.

The truth is that they should have deemed it an honour, as that bureau once supported the shipping charts and maps of none less than a certain Horatio Nelson. It was one of a number of possessions belonging to the *Victory* that Revd Alexander Scott brought to the parish church when he was vicar. Scott was chaplain to Nelson at the Battle of Trafalgar. It was to Scott that the dying Nelson apparently whispered the immortal words: 'Thank God I have done my duty.' And it was Scott who was at his bedside, rubbing his chest to alleviate the pain, when Nelson breathed his last. It is said that Nelson died in the arms of Scott. Ever faithful, Scott even kept watch over the body, day and night, when it lay in state at Greenwich.

On retirement from the navy, Scott was given many of Nelson's personal belongings from the *Victory*. Scott, who lived in the vicarage at nearby Burnham-on-Crouch, where he was also curate, loved Southminster. The people looked fondly upon their war hero too, helping him to raise funds to help the families of those who fell at Trafalgar.

That special bureau from the *Victory* – which Scott is said to have put to good use – along with a number of other artefacts can still be found in the Church of St Leonard.

⚜ STAPLEFORD ABBOTTS ⚜

He has murder in his eyes
The horrific murder of an Essex constable in 1927 became famous throughout the police world.

The investigation broke new ground in the science of ballistics after the culprits were convicted when a gun belonging to one of them was matched with the cartridges found at the scene of the crime.

However, there was something else about the murder that attracted so much attention. After being shot in the head, PC George Gutteridge had both of his eyes shot out.

The belief that the dead can still see is an age-old one. However, it is thought that Frederick Browne, one of two men convicted of murder, fired those two extra bullets for fear that his victim might reveal the identity of his killer. There

A roadside memorial now marks the spot where an infamous murder took place.

was a belief at the time that the last image seen by a person was photographically imprinted on the retinas of the eyes. It is said Browne genuinely believed that the image of him firing the gun was permanently planted in the eyes of PC Gutteridge.

Poor PC Gutteridge was gunned down after stopping the occupants of a stolen car while on his beat at Stapleford Abbotts, near Chigwell. Gutteridge Lane is now named in his honour, and there is a memorial here to mark the spot where he was shot as he got out his notebook for what he thought would be a routine arrest. Both Browne and his accomplice were hanged.

'Day' light robbery

The wife of author Thomas Day could have been forgiven if she had emerged from their farmhouse in Stapleford Abbotts each morning wearing clothes that did not match.

And, no doubt, should she have been the laughing stock of the village, she would still not have reminded her eccentric husband that it was his fault. For it seems the uncomplaining and obedient Mrs Day may have been forced to dress in the dark.

Mr Day, who went on to gain fame for his children's book *The History of Sandford and Merton*, married Esther Milnes in 1778. They obtained a house and a few acres of farmland at Stapleford Abbotts not long after their wedding. However, the house was a near ruin and much renovation work had to be carried out. It is said the room that was to be the master bedroom had to be completely rebuilt and workmen asked Day where he would like the window. It has to be understood that Day was the sort of chap who did not care much for himself or his immediate family, it would seem. He made the welfare of others his chief concern. He was said to be very generous to his farmhands, increasing their wages and repairing their homes. It all meant he was a very busy man and, in response to such a trivial matter as a window, he simply told the workmen he was too busy to care. He said he would have a hole cut in the wall at a later date when he had more time to spare. The astonished workmen are said to have done exactly as they were told, with the result that the master bedroom was built without a window. In the days before electric light, that was not the best of ideas. No doubt the thrifty Day also denied his wife the luxury of a candle and she certainly would not have had a servant to help her dress. In the end, it is said the chamber had to become a lumber-room, rather than the main bedroom of the house.

It seems Mrs Day was a patient and submissive spouse. She would have needed to be. In earlier life, Day attempted to 'train' a wife when he failed to find his perfect match. Many, perhaps not surprisingly, had turned down his proposals. In desperation, he adopted two foundlings from an orphanage who were not even teenagers at the time. He tried to educate them to become perfect wives, but eventually gave up on hearing one of them scream when hot wax was dropped on her arm! You had to be made of stern stuff to be Mrs Day, though Esther – the woman who did eventually fulfil that role – is thought to have shared her husband's vision and willingly adopted his ascetic lifestyle. However, it certainly does not appear to have been a bundle of laughs for her. It is said the writer prevented her from singing and forced her to give up playing the harpsichord, for he believed 'we have no right to luxuries while the poor want bread'.

Thomas Day's aim in life was to improve the working conditions of agricultural labourers. He did help to do that, but it is believed he was not a very successful farmer. His stay at Stapleford Abbotts was not a long one and a move to Surrey soon followed.

⁂ STOCK ⁂

Spider man

You might hear a story in the village of Stock, near Ingatestone, that would perhaps make you think twice about lighting the log fire.

It is not uncommon to find the odd bird up a chimney, but regulars at the Bear inn found something a lot bigger.

In Victorian times, there was an ostler who earned the nickname 'Spider'. He devised an ingenious way of extracting some spare change from the purse of many a traveller. The regulars had seen his disappearing trick more than once before, but those who saw it for the first time could not help but be amazed. Spider would nip up a chimney in one part of the pub and then, as if by magic, reappear out of another fireplace in a different part of the inn. It was no trick, as the two chimneys met, but it still must have required a certain amount of elasticity and suppleness.

No doubt Spider won many a bet with astonished diners, his reward probably being a drink, for it is said he was himself partial to a tipple. In fact, it was reported that Spider would sometimes stay up the chimney for long periods in order to sleep off his hangover. In order to get him to come down, presumably at closing time, the locals would smoke him out by adding some more fuel to the fire. However, on one occasion he did not come down. There are various versions of the tale, but all with the same tragic result – the body of poor Spider was eventually found jammed between the two chimneys. He had suffocated. Needless to say, the ghost of Spider was reported for many a year afterwards, and his appearance on those occasions really would have given the regulars something to be amazed about.

⚜ STONDON MASSEY ⚜

Byrd feathered his own nest

One can only wonder whether famous composer William Byrd felt any pangs of guilt when he moved to Stondon Place in the late sixteenth century.

The house in Stondon Massey, near Chipping Ongar, belonged to the Shelleys – a Catholic family. It was through their misfortune that fellow Catholic Byrd – seen by many as the father of English music – came to live at the once impressive abode. The Shelleys had just had their property confiscated by the Crown due to Mr Shelley's involvement in an alleged popish plot.

While Catholics all over the country were suffering persecution, Byrd – despite his faith – continued to prosper. There must have been a lot of head-scratching among the locals when a man of the same faith as the owners of Stondon Place – effectively ousted for their religion – should turn up on the doorstep in the 1590s as the new tenant. Byrd was presented as a 'papistical recusant'. Indeed, it appears he had not done much to embrace the new Protestant religion. Byrd was regularly fined for recusancy and was suspended from the Chapel Royal for a spell. However, unlike many Catholics, such as Mr Shelley, he escaped severe punishment.

That it was obvious Byrd was a follower of Rome makes it even more ironic that he should, at the same time, be responsible for writing music for the new Church of England, though it has to be said that some of his work was clearly from the pen of a man with Catholic sympathies. The Crown granted Byrd, along with Thomas Tallis, a patent for selling music and, when Tallis died in 1585, Byrd had the monopoly. He wrote music for masses, services, madrigals and songs. If someone wanted music for some words they had penned, Byrd was their man. No doubt it was Byrd's talent that ensured he remained in royal favour. Perhaps his faith was overlooked because of it. Another theory is that among his friends in high places were the Petres of nearby Ingatestone Hall. They were another Catholic family who generally remained in favour during the troubled times. Some even suggest that Byrd was eventually granted special permission to practice his religion under licence during the reign of Queen Elizabeth.

It is more than likely that the Shelleys of Stondon Place could not give two hoots about the talents of Byrd. They did all they could to get their property back, but in vain. Byrd became embroiled in a legal dispute with the widow of Mr Shelley that lasted for years. One can perhaps understand the Shelleys feeling aggrieved. It probably felt like salt had been rubbed into the wound to see one of their own faith occupying their house.

Byrd is now regarded as the greatest Tudor composer – the Shakespeare of music. One can only assume he did not feel too much guilt or sympathy at profiting from the Shelleys' misfortune. He eventually bought the property outright and lived at Stondon Massey for some thirty years in total. It is believed he was buried in the parish church, at his wish, following his death in 1623. Stondon Place had presumably become home sweet home to him – even if it appears to have been with the help of a little preferential treatment.

He needed another nail in the coffin

Residents of Stondon Massey should have known their churchwarden would not rest in peace in the years following his death in 1754.

It seems he was pretty keen to rise from the grave and wasted little time in doing so.

According to a former clergyman of the parish church, who recorded the extraordinary tale, the burial of Richard Jordan was a difficult one. It is said that on several occasions the sexton peered into the Jordan family vault to check that all was as it should be after the funeral. Each time – the clergyman recorded – the corpse was found quite motionless, as you would expect it to be, but outside the coffin! It is not known how many times it was replaced in its box. One has to smile at the idea of the deceased man rising from his coffin and then playing 'dead' when he heard the sexton approach. It might not have been quite like that, but people were spooked enough to put a chain around the coffin to stop Jordan from getting out again.

Some say Richard Jordan is still not at rest in the churchyard at Stondon Massey.

Needless to say, not even chains could prevent the former churchwarden from rising from the grave. Numerous tales emerged of people witnessing the ghost of Richard Jordan hovering among the tombstones in the parish churchyard and elsewhere in the village.

It is said one witness tried to decapitate the spirit with a scythe, but, as he raised the weapon, his swinging arm froze in mid-air as though he was paralysed.

The sceptical would argue that it is hardly surprising such an unusual burial should spark so many ghost stories. No doubt the burial of Richard Jordan may have been slightly exaggerated over the years by superstitious parishioners. In fact, chaining down coffins was not unusual, bodysnatching once being a major inconvenience.

However, the story of such a mysterious burial deserves a ghost to keep it going. In the case of Mr Jordan it seems you cannot keep a good yarn down – or a corpse for that matter!

$\mathcal{T}$

❖ THAXTED ❖

A town made from steel

If things had been a little different, visitors to the delightful town of Thaxted might have been confronted with a sign: Welcome to Thaxted – Town of Steel.

Of course, that honour now sits solely with the city of Sheffield. However, Thaxted was the leading cutlery centre in the south of England during medieval times.

The most famous building in Thaxted – the much-photographed Guildhall – is a visible sign of this once profitable industry. The Guild of Cutlers reputedly built it at the end of the fourteenth century, though some now argue it is from a later date.

The Guildhall at Thaxted reflects a glorious and profitable past.

It is said the cutlers had a hand in the building of the parish church too. One of those it is dedicated to is St Lawrence, the patron saint of cutlers.

Visitors to Thaxted will also see some crossed swords on the town sign, further evidence of this once thriving industry. It was not only swords that were manufactured here. Knives, blade axes, pommels and even surgical instruments came from Thaxted.

The Red Vicar

Compared to most Europeans, the English are a little reserved when it comes to flying flags.

The Revd Conrad Noel was not, however.

The vicar of Thaxted did not simply fly the red cross of St George from his church either. In flying the red flag of socialism, he was nailing his colours to the mast.

The Revd Noel was an eccentric, and a very controversial clergyman. He was perhaps the least famous of a quartet of socialists who made their home in this part of Essex – the society beauty the Countess of Warwick, writer H.G. Wells, and composer Gustav Holst being the other three – but he certainly did not live in their shadow.

It was the influential Countess of Warwick – owner of nearby Easton Lodge – who presented Noel to the living of Thaxted. Holst – who lived in Town Street – became a great friend and ensured the music at the church was probably the best in the country, the composer also training the choir.

Noel was already known for his socialism and unconventionality when he arrived in town. On his appointment to the post in 1910, an anti-socialist group threatened to stone the Bishop of St Albans if he inducted the new vicar. Ecclesiastical disputes over Church ritual and incense soon paled into insignificance when the clergyman started to fly not only the red flag of socialism by the altar, but also the flag of Sinn Féin. Noel did still fly the red cross of St George, but he refused to fly the Union Jack, believing it to be a symbol of imperialism.

A memorial to Revd Conrad Noel can be found in the church that he served in such controversial fashion.

There were many protests, not just locally. The most forceful objectors were a group of Cambridge empire-loyalist students who invaded the church and tore down the flags. The stubborn and determined Noel simply replaced them. Demonstrators came in their hundreds to voice their anger at the vicar, who was only defeated when the dispute went before an ecclesiastical court and he was ordered to take down the offending flags. Ever since, Revd Conrad Noel – who dedicated a chapel in the church to famous socialist rebel John Ball – has been known as the 'Red Vicar' of Thaxted.

Noel remained a controversial figure in Thaxted, but held the post of vicar until his death in 1942. His wife was responsible for restarting the famous tradition of morris dancing in the town, while Holst helped ensure that Whitsuntide Festival at Thaxted became a national event.

The Revd Conrad Noel will always be remembered for his radical politics, but it appears he was a good man and well liked. He was just convinced that politics was part and parcel of the gospel of Christ. Inside his church there is a (perhaps deserved) memorial to Noel, a Thaxted resident who did much for the town, though it is unlikely you will find any flags flying in his honour!

⚜ THEYDON BOIS ⚜

The Scrooge of Essex

John Elwes would often walk from the family farm at Theydon Bois to the capital in order to save the coach fare.

There is perhaps nothing unusual in that. Indeed, many people in the eighteenth century were poor and had no choice but to walk. However, Elwes was not poor and did have a choice. He chose not to call a cab when he needed to be at Smithfield market to sell his cattle – some 17 miles away – simply because he was a miser. It has been suggested that novelist Charles Dickens based Ebenezer Scrooge on John Elwes.

Elwes was very rich. He inherited a fortune when his mother died, but there was more to come. He was also the heir to his uncle and, when he died some ten years later, the nephew inherited his vast estate on the Essex/Suffolk border too, all of which made Elwes one of the richest men in England.

However, the inheritance of his uncle came at a price. Sir Hervey Elwes was a miser too and there is little doubt he was a huge influence on his nephew. It is said the younger Elwes acquired his own stingy habits through years of trying to gain favour with Sir Hervey. He succeeded and the two started to enjoy each other's company. When John first started to visit his uncle at his Stoke by Clare home just over the Essex border in Suffolk, he was a different man. He also had a different name, his own being Meggot. He changed it to 'Elwes' as this was another condition of inheritance set by his uncle.

John Meggot was a bit of a rake and a London dandy. He had no problem spending his money, but his love of it made him fulfil the role – at least when visiting his uncle – of one who was frugal with their cash. On his way to Stoke by Clare, Meggot would stop at a Chelmsford inn and re-emerge a different person. His usual natty attire made way for rags that he knew would win the approval of his uncle. After all, Sir Hervey would be unwilling to leave his money to one who would waste it on pretty clothes. It was said Sir Hervey was so mean that he and his guests went to bed as soon as it was dark to avoid the need of lighting a candle. Dinner was a sparse meal. Uncle and nephew would share some wine – not a bottle but a glass. Meggot would secretly dine before visiting his uncle to avert any pangs of hunger while under his roof.

However, such was his influence that Meggot – perhaps through habit – began to adopt his uncle's ways. By the late 1740s, he is thought to have been a miser himself. He no longer stopped at 'expensive' inns and would carry hard-boiled eggs in his pockets to avoid shelling (excuse the pun) out for a meal.

Despite his reluctance to dip into his pocket on most occasions, Meggot, or perhaps we should again refer to him as Elwes, did sometimes. In fact, he led a contradictory life when it came to money. He thought nothing of gambling with thousands of pounds. It is said he often spent all night gambling and would then turn up at Smithfield the next morning to sell his cattle, fiercely and stubbornly bartering for the last shilling. At times he lived off crumbs, and yet other times he would splash the cash and could be very generous, giving thousands of pounds to strangers, or to finance architectural projects.

Theydon Hall at Theydon Bois, near Epping, was just one of the family residences. Elwes spent most of his life at another of their estates in Berkshire, or in London. It is safe to say that this eccentric would have only afforded himself the luxury of travelling between each estate by coach as the very last resort.

⚜ THEYDON MOUNT

One bride for seven brothers
It is not a good thing if your brother takes a fancy to the girl of your dreams. It is even worse if all six of your brothers do!

That appears to have been the case here, according to a story that emanated from the walls of the once impressive Hill Hall at Theydon Mount, near Epping.

The girl that became the desire of seven brothers is said to have been undecided as to which one to choose as her husband. It seems there was one sure way to find out who the worthiest of the seven was. She is said to have ordered the seven brothers to fight for the right to wed her. The victor would then have proved his love and worth. Sadly, or so the story goes, there was no winner. It is said all seven fought to the death – and none survived. Full of remorse, the young woman put on her bridal gown and killed herself.

There are a number of variations of the legend. Some have suggested that the seven men who died at Hill Hall on that same day hundreds of years ago were, in fact, the brothers of the bride who is said to now haunt the vicinity following her suicide. They did not approve of the new love of her life and each challenged him to a duel. The prospective brother-in-law must have been some man, for it is said he killed all seven brothers one after the other. None too pleased, his bride-to-be obviously decided this act of butchery deserved no prize and took her own life. Whatever version you wish to believe, the moral of the story is that some women are probably not worth fighting over!

⚜ THORNDON ⚜

She who must be obeyed
Men will do most things for a woman.

Sadly for the dashing James Radcliffe, 3rd Earl of Derwentwater, what he was asked to do was to cost him his life.

Mrs Radcliffe was not exactly the nagging wife, but she made it pretty clear that his role was on the battlefield with the English Jacobites in the eighteenth century. Radcliffe had spent his childhood in exile with the young James Stuart, the Old Pretender, who was seen as James III to the Jacobites. In 1715, the Stuarts set out in an attempt to regain the throne and called upon their old friends for assistance. It was a hopeless cause and Radcliffe knew it. It appears he had reservations about joining the Jacobites. However, Mrs Radcliffe was a brave and forceful woman. She is said to have thrown her fan at the feet of her husband, and ordered him to pick it up and give her his sword in return. Then she announced: 'I will take to the field and you can stay at home.'

Radcliffe was a romantic and a rash man. Accused of being a coward by his own wife was too much for him. He returned the fan to her and held his sword aloft. 'God save King James,' he is said to have cried, and then set out for battle.

Needless to say, things did not go well on the battlefield. Radcliffe was taken prisoner and carried to the Tower of London following the ill-fated Battle of Preston. He was accused of treason and condemned to death. Friends begged for mercy and his wife, no doubt feeling more than a little responsible for his predicament, is said to have gone on her knees to George I to beg for the life of her husband. Sadly, it was in vain and poor Radcliffe was executed.

The remains of the courageous Radcliffe now lie in the Roman Catholic chapel that served Thorndon Hall, Ingrave, near Brentwood. The hall, situated

The remains of a chivalrous soldier were laid to rest at Thorndon Hall.

on the edge of Thorndon Country Park, was once in the hands of the Petres, a prominent Catholic family. Those very remains of the faithful and loyal Radcliffe are perhaps a reminder that *she* should *not* always be obeyed!

⁙ THORPE-LE-SOKEN ⁙

The real Jack or just a ripping yarn?
There is a theory – albeit a highly improbable one – that eminent Victorian physician Sir William Gull does not lie in a grave at Thorpe-le-Soken, near Clacton-on-Sea. Indeed, some have suggested that only stones fill the coffin that was laid to rest here in 1890.

The reason for the theory is an even more staggering theory, one that suggests that Sir William Gull was none other than Jack the Ripper. It has been claimed that Gull murdered the Whitechapel prostitutes as part of a royal conspiracy. Gull died soon after the murders, though some believe it was he who carried out the grisly crimes before he was himself hidden away in an asylum, a funeral and subsequent burial conducted at Thorpe-le-Soken to throw all off the scent.

Was Sir William Gull the notorious Jack the Ripper?

It is only a theory and only a few now believe it may be the truth. However, it is a theory that has inspired countless books and films. When the identity of Jack the Ripper has been revealed in works of fiction, it is Sir William Gull, more than any other on the long list of suspects, who usually turns out to be the murderer, even though he never physically fitted the description of the killer.

The most common theory as to the identity of Jack the Ripper is the one that involves the British royal family, probably because it is the most outrageous of the lot. Gull was physician to Queen Victoria at the time of the murders. It is perhaps a little sad that he should be implicated in something so terrible, something he more than likely had nothing whatsoever to do with. In fact, Gull did much good in his time and enjoyed a celebrated career within royal circles. It was he who successfully treated the Prince of Wales in 1871 when he was on the brink of death following a bout of typhoid.

However, Gull will forever be linked with the conspiracy to protect one of the members of the royal family. It is said that Prince Albert Victor, the monarch's grandson, regularly frequented the slums of the East End. Here he met the working-class Annie Crook. When she became pregnant through him, Her Majesty was not amused. Something had to be done to keep it quiet. The theory is that Annie was locked up in a lunatic asylum. Mary Kelly, one of the victims of Jack the Ripper, was caring for the 'royal' baby when Annie was supposedly kidnapped. Told to keep her mouth shut, she was unable to do so, sealing her own fate and those of her friends who also shared her secret. The few women who knew about the relationship between the prince and Annie Crook had to be silenced, and Gull was theoretically given the task. He made the crimes look like they were the work of a frenzied madman, though there was no doubt that the murderer had more than a little knowledge of all things medical. Once Gull had served his purpose, he was himself supposedly locked away, his secret going to the grave with him. For a few, it is just a question of … which grave?

❧ TILBURY ❧

It's just not cricket

The famous Tilbury Fort has never seen any action – apart from a game of cricket.

However, this turned out to be no ordinary game of cricket and it resulted in the biggest battle ever seen in these parts. It was also arguably the most violent game of cricket in the history of the sport.

There has been a fort at Tilbury since the sixteenth century, its chief job being to guard the approach up the Thames to the capital. However, by the time of this particular game – in 1776 – the fort had seen better days and was in decline, now an inactive military post. The match itself took place on a green just outside its walls and, no doubt, some of the guards would have been among the spectators, the drudgery of their working day broken by the excitement of this unusual spectacle on their doorstep.

A team from Essex were to 'welcome' a team from Kent. The visitors arrived from the other side of the Thames via rowing boats. They were probably greeted

Tilbury Fort's guns still point across the Thames to Kent ... and maybe for good reason.

warmly, but it is said one of the Essex men suggested one of the opponents was not from the county of Kent. That was simply not cricket! An argument ensued and Essex refused to play unless that rogue individual, who presumably hailed from another county, was dropped from the team. Kent refused and soon fists were raised. It was not long before the two teams were involved in a running battle. They were so full of fury, it is said one of the Kent players rushed across the drawbridge of the fort and entered the guardhouse. Reaching for a musket, he returned to the scene of battle and fired the weapon. It is said one of the Essex players was hit and killed. Further riled, the Essex players went in search of weapons for themselves and both teams grabbed whatever they could find at the fort. There were so few guards on duty that they could do little to stop the riot. Apparently there were further casualties before the Kent team scrambled into their boats and rowed back across the Thames.

The story first appeared in a regional newspaper of the time, but it is not known if any of the cricketers were ever punished, or even apprehended, and some have even denied the story's authenticity. If it is true it would indeed be the only time Tilbury Fort has seen any serious fighting, and it might be that the guns still pointing towards the Thames are actually aimed not at those who might come up the river, but at those from across it!

Defoe was the author of his own misfortune
It is a good job Daniel Defoe was an excellent writer.

He was certainly not a good businessman or politician by all accounts.
His life as a novelist is well documented, but his career in business and politics is something of a mystery. What we do know is that his many enterprises away from the study would not have been the first thing to make it onto his CV.

It is believed Defoe moved to Tilbury, not too far from its famous fort, in the mid-1690s. He established a tile factory, at its peak employing more than 100 people. However, it is a wonder he had any staff at all, as he did not appear to treat his employees very well. In fact, he admitted that at one time he was forced to employ casual labourers and beggars who happened to be in the area, though even that proved difficult. His reluctance to dip too far into his pocket seemed to be the reason few wanted to work for him. Defoe recorded that when he 'offered nine shillings a week to strolling fellows at my door, they have frequently told me to my face, they could get more a-begging; and I once set a lusty fellow in the stocks for making the experiment'.

Defoe ensured he himself at least lived in style at Tilbury. He owned a farmstead, his fine house close to the river where he had a pleasure boat. Ever the entrepreneur, he rented out some of his land, but he did not appear to be the greatest landlord either. One of his tenants sued him on at least one occasion.

The tile factory suffered because of poor management on Defoe's part, but also because of the poor quality of the product. His roof tiles were not in the same league as those produced by the Dutch and were said to be unable to protect houses in extreme weather. Defoe was eventually put out of business and is said to have lost thousands of pounds in the venture. It was not the only time one of his enterprises failed. Defoe was declared bankrupt on at least two occasions, once as a hosier. To be fair to him, the writer did make a go of his tile factory and it did flourish initially, but it is said he neglected his business, possibly to concentrate on his writing. The factory was forever beset by problems and Defoe was not the greatest at customer – or employee – relations.

Politically, Defoe also had a tough time at Tilbury. The scribe was a lifelong Presbyterian. It was while here that he penned his famous satire *The Shortest Way with the Dissenters*, which was published in 1702. The pamphlet pretended to put forward an argument for wiping out dissenters, Defoe being among them. It was really an attack on the High Church Tories. However, none of the political parties, or Queen Anne, was impressed. In fact, the work caused outrage. Defoe was arrested on publication and imprisoned. He continued to write satires from behind bars, though it is said this enforced spell away from his Tilbury factory was the beginning of the end of that enterprise, if it had not already been doomed.

The prolific Daniel Defoe went on to pen numerous political pamphlets and some memorable novels, such as *Robinson Crusoe* and *Moll Flanders*, the latter being set in Essex, but it seems his business sense never improved with the passing of years. He died in 1731 – on the run from his creditors!

✤ TOLLESHUNT D'ARCY ✤

The diary of John Henry Salter

It takes a lot of dedication and discipline to keep a diary.

John Henry Salter, an extrovert doctor, would have certainly had those traits in abundance.

He started his diary at the age of eight and only his death – in his ninety-first year – brought it to a halt. It was a diary to put those from the pens of Samuel Pepys and John Evelyn in the shade. This incredible work, covering some 30,000 days, filled eighty volumes and consisted of more than 10 million words!

It is fair to say that the diary of Dr Salter cannot be described as the greatest contribution to English literature, but this eccentric physician's life's work

Salter went in search of game on Tollesbury Wick marshes.

– not surprisingly, it was published in abridged form – offers the reader an intriguing insight into a very full life.

Salter came to Tolleshunt D'Arcy, a village near Maldon, in 1864. He was in his twenties when he took over the practice there and soon became a very popular figure. It is perhaps a surprise he had any time to care for the villagers or even to pen his diary. He was a man who loved adventure. He travelled the world in search of thrills. He was particularly fond of shooting big game and it is recorded that he shot bears in Russia while in the company of the Tsar. On another occasion, having no suitable trousers to wear, he went hunting wolves in the snows of Russia wearing his pyjamas. Salter went in search of game on Tollesbury Wick marshes too. On one particular day, he shot so many birds that the wagon bringing them home collapsed. Despite his willingness to shoot animals, he was fond of them. He bred dogs and became a judge at prestigious shows.

Salter was a caring and kind man, but you would not have wanted to make him angry. Among his many talents, he was also a top bare-knuckle fighter. In his early days, a bout with a gypsy cost him his right eye, which he had removed and replaced with a glass alternative.

The home of the eccentric diarist John Henry Salter.

Despite his many interests, Salter did not neglect his patients. He is reputed to have brought some 7,000 children into the world. He also carried out numerous operations before the days of anaesthetics. There was no amazing secret to his zest for life. He wrote: 'I have discovered how to keep well. I never have more than two meals, with nothing to eat or drink between. I go to bed at night, and wake up five hours later as sure as clockwork. The rest of the day I work.'

And work and play this outgoing medical man most certainly did.

Salter was laid to rest in the cemetery on the corner of Beckingham Road. Lying there also is another person who penned lots of words. In fact, novelist Margery Allingham later lived in Dr Salter's old home – D'Arcy House. In the literary world, she was far more successful than the physician. More successful maybe, but not quite as prolific!

$$\mathcal{U}$$

❖ ULTING ❖

Friends in high places

It is strange that celebrated Victorian balloonist Joseph Simmons should be killed so close to the home of the man he made history with only a few years earlier.

Simmons died when his balloon crashed in a field at Ulting, almost within shouting distance of the Great Totham home of the eccentric Sir Claude Champion de Crespigny.

The two men had become the first to cross the North Sea in a balloon. Sir Claude was a sportsman and adventurer. Ballooning was just one of the many activities he took up. In 1882, he joined Simmons in an attempt to cross the Channel. The duo was due to set off from nearby Maldon. However, it had taken so long to inflate the balloon that the wind had got up to a dangerous level. Simmons advised his friend to abort the trip, but Sir Claude refused, perhaps feeling he could not disappoint the huge paying crowd that had gathered to watch the momentous lift-off. It was certainly a memorable moment. As the balloon was preparing to ascend, a gust of wind caught it and the basket was dragged across the field, hitting a brick wall. Sir Claude broke his leg, but the balloon, without him inside the basket, managed to rise again and Simmons successfully landed it in France.

The disappointed Sir Claude was not to be outdone. In the following year, the duo was back at Maldon attempting to take a balloon over the North Sea. This time the pair was successful, making history when they touched down in Holland.

However, some five years after that memorable day, Simmons was to meet his end attempting a flight from London to Vienna. Sir Claude was not with him on this occasion, no doubt having become bored of ballooning and looking for a new challenge elsewhere. Of all the places Simmons could have crashed, it is incredible to think he would end his days almost on the doorstep of his old friend Sir Claude. Due to unfavourable winds, Simmons decided to abandon his attempt not long after setting off from the capital. Some have suggested he may have deliberately chosen to land in Essex – and close to the home of Sir Claude – as he would have known the area. The theory

Ulting, with its pretty riverside church, was where a famous balloonist met his fate.

will forever remain just that, however. Most believe it to have been pure coincidence. It is said Simmons, in a bid to avoid houses, only sought a suitable field in which to land. Sadly, the man who had cheated death so many times was unable to do so on this occasion. As the balloon descended, it is said to have hit some trees and then soared into the air before bursting, throwing the occupants to the ground. Simmons and his two passengers lay unconscious. Sadly, the former died at the scene.

Ballooning was, of course, a dangerous pastime back then. Simmons and Sir Claude knew the risks. Not that the latter would be put off by that. Sir Claude had a reputation for being something of a daredevil. He would attempt anything to prove his courage and actively went in search of danger. Among his other interests were swimming rapids, big-game hunting and steeplechasing, Sir Claude building a racecourse in the fields surrounding his home – the aptly named Champion Lodge – to satisfy the latter passion. He also liked a fight. It is said his male servants had to prove their worth by facing him in the 'ring' before they were offered a job.

Fortunately for Sir Claude, unlike Simmons he did manage to live to a decent age, despite the risks he took.

WALTHAM ABBEY

Take up your cross and follow me

Many have come from far and wide to take in the delights of Waltham Abbey over the years – including the four-legged variety. In the first half of the eleventh century, two dozen cattle certainly decided it was the place to be. Known simply as Waltham then, these particular beasts of the field made the long trek from Somerset, and were ultimately responsible for the building of the once great abbey that gave the town its suffix.

It all started in the 1030s when a blacksmith in the Somerset village of Montacute discovered a large flint cross with a carved figure of Christ on it. Tovi, the lord of the manor, decided it should be taken to one of the great holy sites, such as Canterbury or Winchester. And so it was loaded onto a wagon ready for the journey. However, the twelve red oxen and twelve white cows charged with the job of pulling that wagon had other ideas. It is said that they refused to budge. It was only when the frustrated Tovi announced he was going back to Waltham – where he owned a hunting lodge – that the beasts suddenly started to move. According to this fanciful tale, the cattle – unguided – did not stop until they reached that seemingly desirable location, whereupon Tovi decided to build a church to house the cross. The story attracted much interest and soon Waltham became a centre of pilgrimage. People flocked to touch the cross that was said to possess miraculous powers. The cross became famous and one of those who paid it a visit was a man named Harold. He was reputedly cured of paralysis on praying beneath the cross in about 1060. He was so thrilled that he ordered a new, larger church to be built on the site, a building worthy to house such a holy object. Some six years later that same man became King of England. It is said that Harold II, as he was now known, also stopped off at Waltham Abbey on his way to meet William of Normandy at the Battle of Hastings. Once again, according to legend, he prayed beneath the cross, but this time the figure of Christ bowed its head. It was taken to be an ill omen. Harold came back to Waltham Abbey, but not alive. After receiving that infamous arrow in the eye, the body of the king was identified by his mistress and then carried home by some of the abbey

Waltham Abbey is reputed to be the final resting place of King Harold II.

monks. It is said Harold was buried at Waltham Abbey and a stone now marks his supposed resting place. As for the cross, it was seemingly lost following the Dissolution of the Monasteries in the sixteenth century.

The king who gave the abbot food for thought
Friar Tuck – thanks to his name and image – is so often viewed to be the archetypal man of the habit.

Certainly, the holy men of the abbeys and monasteries of England had a reputation for liking their nosh – and plenty of it. No doubt, more than a few would have been as plump as the legendary associate of Robin Hood.

At the time of the Dissolution of the Monasteries, the great religious houses had become very wealthy, and so had those who resided within their walls. Needless to say, the gluttonous monks did not go without.

Henry VIII played a trick on one of the abbots at Waltham Abbey.

Waltham Abbey was no different. However, Henry VIII must have had a soft spot for the old place. It was one of the last English religious houses to be dissolved in the sixteenth century.

Henry is believed to have been a frequent visitor. However, there is a charming legend that he was not recognised by one of the abbots when he came on one occasion. As Henry – himself partial to a good feast – tucked in during a lavish supper, this particular abbot complained that he could not enjoy his food, as he was prone to suffering from indigestion. He went further to declare that he would give £100 to have an appetite as good as the guest before him.

It was said that Henry had the abbot kidnapped shortly after his visit. The confused holy man was thrown into the Tower and fed on a diet of bread and water. After a short time, much to the surprise of the abbot, he was invited to feast on a magnificent supper in place of his usual prison grub. The now ravenous abbot set about demolishing the contents of his plate like he had never done before. And as he finished – no doubt rubbing his bulging stomach in satisfaction – the king walked in and demanded his £100!

Don't fall asleep on the job

Falling asleep on the job does not usually have dire consequences. At worst you might get a warning from the boss not to do it again. If you worked at the Royal Gunpowder Mills at Waltham Abbey, you would not have had a chance to do it again. You would have been blown to smithereens.

From the mid-nineteenth century, new nitro-based explosives and propellants were developed to replace gunpowder that had been produced here since the 1660s.

Creating the chemical reaction required to produce nitroglycerin was a risky business. Should the mixture become too hot or too cold, it was likely to explode. Without any computers, the very boring – but extremely dangerous – job of keeping an eye on the thermometer was left to an individual. It was a round-the-clock operation and vital that the man charged with watching the mercury, to check it did not rise or fall, did not fall asleep. To help him concentrate, he was a given a one-legged stool. Should he begin to drop off he would literally drop off! However, sustaining a bruise or two from falling off the stool would have been a small price to pay.

Employees at the Royal Gunpowder Mills had to be very careful. It is unlikely you would have seen workers sporting long hair or a bushy beard. That was against the rules. Should even a tiny grain of sand or other speck of dirt become trapped in hair and then fall into the mixture during the mixing process, it could have sparked an explosion. Even tools used here could not be made of iron or steel, as those metals can create sparks when hit or dropped.

These are just some of the many fascinating tales to emerge from the Royal Gunpowder Mills at Waltham Abbey. What went on behind closed doors is only just coming to light. For some 300 years, the activities here were a national

The Royal Gunpowder Mills at Waltham Abbey had its own canal system to transport explosive materials.

secret and many did not even know of its existence. Novelist H.G. Wells, a one-time Essex resident, certainly knew of it. In *The War of the Worlds*, he wrote: 'Here [at Chelmsford] there were rumours of Martians at Epping, and news of the destruction of Waltham Abbey Powder Mills in a vain attempt to blow up one of the invaders.'

The Royal Gunpowder Mills at Waltham Abbey continued to play a major role in the twentieth century. During the two World Wars, it produced cordite – the now preferred propellant – and, for the first two years of the Second World War, was the sole producer of RDX, the explosive used in the bouncing bombs of the Dambusters. By the late twentieth century, the site had become an important research facility for rocket propulsion. It is now a tourist attraction.

The complex at Waltham Abbey, complete with its own canal system to transport the highly dangerous materials, was one of only three royal gunpowder mills in Britain and Ireland. It is now the only site to have survived virtually intact. The Crown purchased it in 1787, and gunpowder produced at Waltham Abbey was once considered to be among the best in the world. Its gunpowder and nitro-based explosives have played a significant part in the rise of Britain as an international power.

Sadly, many lost their lives in the production process, such was the nature of the industry. No doubt that list would have been even longer if it had not been for that one-legged stool.

⚜ WEELEY ⚜

Killed off duty

Every soldier knows he is in a risky business. However, you do not expect to meet your fate at the hands of those people you are supposed to be fighting for. Poor Alexander McDonald of the Cameron Highlanders did.

During the Napoleonic Wars, troops from all over the country were moved to the Essex coast in anticipation of an attack from the Continent. McDonald was indeed the victim of an attack, but from the locals.

It is believed that McDonald and his fellow Scots were stationed near Weeley, north of Clacton-on-Sea. At least, that is where he was laid to rest after the tragic incident. The Highlanders were off duty and decided to head for Little Clacton to visit St James' Day Fair. No doubt the local girls were more than a little impressed when the strangers in military uniform descended on their patch. However, the local male population were not so impressed that their potential sweethearts were now paying no attention to them. No doubt after much consumption of alcohol, there was an inevitable confrontation and it is said that the locals chased the Highlanders out of town. Sadly, McDonald hurt his leg in the fracas and got separated from his fellow soldiers. The angry villagers decided to give him a beating, but went too far and McDonald was killed in the process.

It was a cruel end for poor McDonald, who had lost his life at the hands of those he had come to protect.

It is said that for many years after the death of McDonald, there remained a hole in the roadside close to the Blacksmith's Arms. It is believed the hole was caused when the unfortunate soldier hit his head on the ground. All attempts to fill it apparently were in vain. That is not a particularly fitting monument to McDonald but, fortunately, a more appropriate one can be found in the churchyard at Weeley. It is said the Cameron Highlanders still come to tend his tomb and pay their respects.

⚜ WETHERSFIELD ⚜

Withering lows to Wuthering Heights

If a former curate at Wethersfield had gone on to marry his first love, it is quite possible that *Wuthering Heights* would have been set in flat Essex.

It may be stretching the imagination a little, but Revd Patrick Brontë might have settled in this particular village, near Braintree, rather than Haworth and the moors made famous by daughter Emily, author of one of the most celebrated novels in English literature.

Of course, fate intervened and Emily's mother was Maria Branwell and not Mary Burder, the woman Brontë first fell in love with.

Patrick Brontë came to Wethersfield after studying at Cambridge. He stayed less than three years. On his arrival in 1806, he lodged at a house opposite the church he served. It was in this house – the kitchen to be precise – that he first set eyes on the pretty niece of his landlady. Mary was a frequent visitor and on this occasion had brought her aunt some fresh game that she was busy preparing when the curate walked in. It was apparently love at first sight.

Love blossomed, but it is said that Mary's family were suspicious of her suitor. Brontë was an Irishman and also an Anglican. They were Nonconformists. It appears they were so opposed to the match that Mary was removed from the sight of Brontë, taking lodgings at the home of an uncle in another village. It is said that Brontë continued to write to her, but his letters were intercepted. It is quite possible that Mary believed Brontë no longer cared for her and it is certainly the case that Brontë believed she no longer cared for him. When Mary returned to Wethersfield, the curate had gone, having taken up a new position in Shropshire. It is said he left his portrait with the words: 'Mary, you have torn the heart; spare the face.' It could have almost been the tragic plot of a Brontë novel!

The exact reason why the relationship did not end in marriage is not really known. However, there was one final twist, some fourteen years later. Brontë wrote to his first love again after the death of his wife Maria. He had been left to bring up six young children and was in the market for a new spouse. Mary was still single, but wrote to tell him that she wanted nothing more to do with the man who presumably broke her heart – a man now in his mid-forties with half a dozen children. She also declined his suggestion of a reunion at Wethersfield.

As for Mary, she eventually did find a new love and married him. Patrick Brontë never remarried, though his daughters did not do too badly without a mother to bring them up!

⚜ WILLINGALE ⚜

Rivals were still able to sing from the same hymn sheet
If you had stood in the middle of the churchyard at Willingale, near Chipping Ongar, in days gone by you could have enjoyed two Sunday services – simultaneously.

While most villages can boast a church, this particular village can boast two. However, what is more surprising is that the two share the same churchyard. The reason for the oddity is not known, though there are, as you would expect, plenty of theories.

Two churches share one churchyard at Willingale.

The two churches represented the parishes of Willingale Doe and Willingale Spain, their names stemming from landowners. Some suggested the said individuals were rivals and that they would not set foot in a church built by the other. In a variation of the same story, the churches are said to be the work of feuding sisters who each attempted to outdo the other.

As delightful as these stories are, they appear to be fiction, as the churches date from different periods. St Andrew's Church in Willingale Spain is thought to date from at least the twelfth century, while St Christopher's Church was built two centuries later.

Sadly, it is no longer possible to listen to two services at the same time, as the villagers, whatever their differences might have been in the past, are united these days and it is only St Christopher's that they now visit to receive their weekly spiritual nourishment.

⁓ WITHAM ⁓

Cat woman
If Witham residents had wanted to fraternise with the local celebrity, it would have helped if they liked cats.

It is said that crime writer Dorothy L. Sayers was too busy with her work to take an active role in Witham life when she moved to the town in 1929. However, she would no doubt have always found time to have a chat about her feline friends. In fact, in a letter she wrote to fellow scribe C.S. Lewis in 1953, while discussing religion and science, she dropped in the fact that she regarded scientist Fred Hoyle with the 'utmost suspicion, for he has publicly announced that he does not like cats'.

Dorothy loved cats and they feature in much of her work and private letters. Writing to her son

Author Dorothy L. Sayers and one of her cats take pride of place in Witham.

in 1930, she spoke of her 'clever' cat Adelbert that would 'run after balls of paper and bring them back to you to throw, just like a dog'. Another pet cat was named Peter after Lord Peter Wimsey, her famous aristocrat detective. In another letter, she wrote of her surprise when Peter – the cat – had kittens!

Dorothy liked nothing better than talking about cats, and her letters were sometimes adorned with sketches of them. It is not thought that Dorothy was

The Witham home of Dorothy L. Sayers and her many feline friends.

particularly fond of animals – she had no interest in country matters – but she did, as well as keeping many cats, raise pigs in her backyard at Witham, one of which she immortalised in a frivolous Christmas poem. She suggested that the lot of a pig was not a good one and it was far better to be a cat:'Since, though he bulge with fish and meat, he never will be fit to eat.' No doubt the cats belonging to the author – such was her love for them – were particularly fortunate.

Dorothy L. Sayers lived in a house in Newland Street until her death in 1957. There is a statue of the author on the opposite side of the road. Few pets of the famous have been immortalised in bronze or stone, but one stands at her feet here. It is said that one of her cats actually followed her around the town, so it is therefore only fitting she should be depicted with one by her side.

⚜ WOODHAM FERRERS ⚜

As the hostess said to the archbishop

If there had been tabloid newspapers in the late sixteenth century there is little doubt Edwin Sandys would have been front-page news on one occasion.

He was caught in bed with a married woman. That is not good under normal circumstances, but Sandys was also the Archbishop of York at the time!

Sandys, whose family residence was at Woodham Ferrers, north of South Woodham Ferrers, was actually an innocent party in the whole scandal, the victim of a conspiracy to ruin him.

Archbishop Sandys was already in his sixties at the time of the incident in the early 1580s. He was lodging at an inn in Yorkshire and was no doubt accustomed to having a nice hot drink to help him sleep at night. On this occasion, the hostess of the establishment brought it to his room. The archbishop was already snuggled up in bed. Instead of leaving the room after bringing him his mug of cocoa, the hostess jumped in bed alongside him. At that very moment – in the style of a traditional British farce – the husband of the hostess entered, along with a convenient witness. The host of the tavern reached for his dagger and poor Sandys must have at first feared for his life. However, the 'third party' who had witnessed the incident just happened to be Robert Stapleton, a man known to Sandys. He is believed to have been responsible for plotting the conspiracy to ruin the archbishop and it was he, no doubt, who 'calmed' the 'enraged' host whom he had probably paid well for the use of his considerable acting abilities. Stapleton then set about advising the confused and frightened Sandys that it would perhaps be best if the whole incident did not come to the attention of the public. Though the archbishop was innocent, it did not look good and many might not have believed even a man of God. And so Sandys resorted to bribery in order to keep the sorry affair out of the public domain. However, eventually he could take no more – or at least his purse could not. He decided to end the extortion, even if it meant the incident coming to light. Despite knowing his public career was in danger, Sandys decided to report the sorry saga to none other than Queen Elizabeth herself.

The case went before the Star Chamber. Fortunately for Sandys, the conspirators received their comeuppance and the archbishop was allowed to remain in his post, though the stigma, it is said, never really left him.

The Woodham Ferrers home of Sandys, which he built, is now called Edwin's Hall in honour of its former resident.

⚜ WORMINGFORD ⚜

Here be dragons
Every Englishman knows the legend of St George and the dragon.

However, not so many know that a village in Essex, close to the border of Suffolk, is where the brave knight saw off the fire-breathing beast – apparently. In fact, you can still see a mysterious mound in Wormingford, the body of the dragon supposedly buried beneath. The word 'worm' actually comes from an old term for a serpent or dragon, backing up the claim that the legendary beast was defeated at what became Wormingford – the 'ford of the worm'.

There are many stories to which locals can turn in order to claim St George and his dragon for their own. One version of the legend suggests the beast was not a dragon, but a crocodile, and that St George – the dragon slayer – lived much later than the era in which most historians place the patron saint of England, the man usually credited with slaying a dragon. In the twelfth century, Richard I, after returning from one of his crusades, is said to have brought back a small crocodile. The peculiar reptile was housed in the royal menagerie at the Tower of London. However, the creature grew larger and larger until it one day managed to escape from its cage. It supposedly made its way down the Thames and then turned inland until it reached these parts.

The villagers were terrified when it appeared in their midst and were probably not even sure what it was. It is quite possible they mistook it for a dragon. After sacrificing a few maidens in the hope it would be satisfied and retreat to where it had come from, they soon realised it was not going to leave in a hurry.

In desperation, they called upon their lord, Sir George, to dispose of it. The courageous knight put on his armour and took up his lance, tracking down the beast and killing it. There is also a similar legend involving another Sir George of Wormingford from an even later era.

Truth or fiction, the village is clearly proud of its association with 'dragons'. Not many parish churches can boast a stained-glass window that depicts a crocodile munching one of its unfortunate victims!

❧ WRITTLE ❧

The birth of British broadcasting

It was not a case of all eyes on Writtle at 8 p.m. on Valentine's Day in 1922 – but all ears.

This pretty village, with its archetypal green and duck pond, was the unlikely birthplace of British broadcasting.

The pretty village of Writtle was the unlikely birthplace of British broadcasting.

It was from an ex-army hut not too far from the village green that regular radio broadcasting began. With its 'Two Emma Toc' call sign, 2MT Writtle became the forerunner to the BBC. In fact, even when that particular organisation was founded later in the year, people were reluctant to switch channels. The Writtle radio station even had the audacity to broadcast brief satirical sketches to mock the new rival. The public loved it and could not get enough of it. Unfortunately, 2MT was only granted a licence to broadcast for half-an-hour once a week. Listeners held the show in such high regard that it is said they even asked the BBC to close down for the 30 minutes 2MT was on air to ensure there was no interference with the signal.

The first 30-minute shows from Writtle every Tuesday started as simple programmes, consisting of records being played on a gramophone. However, it was not long before this gave way to live broadcasts, which included plays and appearances from some of the world's top singers.

People struggled to get their heads around the technology produced by the famous Marconi Company, which had its base in nearby Chelmsford. It is said guest tenor Lauritz Melchior shattered the microphone on one occasion. He believed he had to sing louder than he had ever sung before in order to be heard back in his native Denmark!

It was not long before presenter Captain P.P. Eckersley became Britain's first radio star. He knew how to captivate an audience and there was never a dull moment when he was on air. Eckersley left to become chief engineer at the BBC, taking a number of his fellow Writtle trailblazers with him. It was not long before the BBC started to grow into the world-famous broadcasting service we know today and soon the airwaves fell silent in Writtle, with 2MT closing in 1923. The Marconi Hut from which those historical broadcasts were made is now housed at Sandford Mill, a museum of science, on the other side of Chelmsford. The site at Writtle now houses flats, which are named after Dame Nellie Melba. It was she who was responsible for the first advertised public broadcast from the Marconi headquarters in New Street, Chelmsford, as early as 1920. However, it was not until 2MT hit the airwaves that British broadcasting entertainment really took off.

So, from Writtle, Essex – a county full of curiosities – it is over and out.

Lightning Source UK Ltd.
Milton Keynes UK
UKOW06f0328150916

283031UK00001B/9/P